Bridges &
Cupolas

by Janet and Richard Strombeck

Illustrated by Marlene Ekman

This book is dedicated to Pernilla, Pauline, and Hilding, the survivors of an earlier generation, who have given us values, sustenance, and encouragement for our efforts.

TABLE OF CONTENTS

SUN DESIGNS
BRIDGES & CUPOLAS

Published by . . . . .Sun Designs
Rexstrom Co., Inc.
P.O. Box 206
Delafield, WI 53018
Tel. 414-567-4255

Authors. . . . . .Janet A. Strombeck
Richard H. Strombeck

Cupola Designs . . . . .Marlene Ekman
James Klopp
Sue Wamsley

Bridge Designs . . . . .Marlene Ekman
James Klopp
Brad Traver

Engineering . . . . .John Bronsted

Drafting . . . . .Albert Park
James Klopp
Lorence Schnur

Acknowledgements

We would like to acknowledge our gratitude for the help from people we can only identify as the American public library system; Ann Tomasic for her help in editing; Hal Bolk for his patience and technical talents; Old House Journal and Harper and Row for permission to use excerpts from their books and publications; and our many customers who have helped make this book possible.

Reference

American Barns & Covered Bridges — Eric Sloane

World's Great Bridges — H.S. Smith

Kissing Bridges — Peterson/Allen

Early American Life Magazine Bridges — Corbett/Rosenblum

Diary of An Early American Boy — Eric Sloane

An Age of Barns — Eric Sloane

Old House Journal

English Garden Ornament — Paul Edwards

FOREWORD

When we first began talking of publishing a series of Study Plan Books several years ago, three things I felt were a "must" for us to do were cupolas, covered bridges and open foot bridges. This was in keeping with our overall program of publishing vanishing, hard-to-find designs and plans of things we personally liked.

I think my first attachment for covered bridges began when my six children were still quite young and we spent some very pleasant "days off" by a covered bridge spanning a river in southern Wisconsin. The special memories I have of these quiet times, away from the noise and traffic, picnicing or walking in the rich fall colors and clean brisk air, has left a permanent impression on me.

In addition to the memories of earlier times, I am one of the many people who are sad to see the passing of these historic, early American covered bridges from the American scene. I also believe many people would again build replicas of these bridges for their own use if reasonable and good construction plans were available. So, it was an "early on" favorite for one of our books.

But what bridge plan book would be complete without a comprehensive selection of colorful open foot bridges for giving character to where you live. Whether you are spanning a stream, decorating a garden, crossing a ravine, or a walkway between buildings, we hope you find a design you like. Some of them are a design composite from people who have written us with their requests. I appreciate all of the letters and the nice comments about our earlier books.

Our interest in cupola designs paralleled that of gazebos. We were interested in having a cupola, but were totally disenchanted with the sterile, assembly-line designs promoted by chain stores in their basic "one design for all" philosophy. That, and a strong interest in unique, well-designed cupolas from our earlier customers, prompted us to combine these designs with the bridges. Historically, the bridges and cupolas were functionally and decoratively associated with early America, and we think our designers Jim Klopp, Marlene Ekman, Brad Traver, Suanne Wamsley, and engineer John Bronsted have done an excellent job in developing a variety of good designs that capture the Early American spirit and our "reverence for wood".

We have also included a little history on each subject from research done by my husband Richard. We hope you will enjoy the story along with the illustrations. We have enjoyed bringing it to you.

INTRODUCTION

This book is a reflection of the attitudes on style, of the people at Sun Designs, and many of our customers who have written or called with their opinions on subject matter and design.

This Study Plan Book contains 36 drawings of cupolas, 21 illustrations of foot bridges, eight covered bridges, and a small amount of history on each subject.

I believe we have presented you with a comprehensive selection of all the subjects, to satisfy almost everyone's taste. This does not preclude you from individualizing these designs further with colors, initials, logos, figure designs, or landscaping in the case of the bridges. I know your imagination will start when you begin looking through this book, as to the design applications to your home and property.

The bridges have all been sized for foot traffic, not vehicles, and designed for practical economy. No changes in bridge sizes or specifications should be done without the advice of an architect or engineer, unless it is an alternate railing design or something inconsequential of that nature. Load limits are shown on (all) bridge illustrations and are explained as follows:

The structural load limit on all bridges are calculated at a minimum of 100#'s per square foot, and the deck board load is calculated at 150#'s per square foot. To more graphically explain the structural load limit, we have indicated on the illustrations, the number of 175# people the bridge will hold if all of the people are equally spaced over the bridge. Bridge illustrations show overall deck dimensions. Stress load engineering data is included with each bridge plan, in case you are interested.

The height dimension shown on the cupola illustrations is measured from the ridge line of the roof to the highest point of the cupola. The ridge line is the highest point, or peak of the roof, shown as the inverted V on the bottom of the cupola. The widths of the cupolas are measured either from side to side or from corner point to corner point in some of the polygonal designs.

Completely detailed construction drawings showing foundation, construction section, elevation, special connection details, construction materials and dimensions have been professionally prepared for each design. The price of each plan is on page 104. Included with each set of plans is an itemized "bill of materials" guide. Types, sizes, amounts, grades, materials source, and material alternates are listed, along with a short glossary of terms and abbreviations used on the plans. I suggest you check local zoning requirements before beginning construction.

Janet A. Strombeck

WEIGHT CAPACITY

* This is the number of people the bridge can hold, *if the* people are evenly disbursed on the bridge (equal distance from each other). You *cannot* put this number of people in one spot. Calculated at 175 lbs. per person. Bridges are for foot traffic only, or a small garden tractor—*no* cars or heavy tractors allowed.

WOOD

A part of Our American Heritage

When our forefathers came to this country, America was a land of beautiful virgin forests, sparkling clear streams, fertile prairies and breathtaking mountains.

As they began to put their roots into this good land, the forest was literally the "life" of their settlements. They knew that not only did their home, barn, fences, bridges, barrels, rakes, locks, nails, hinges, furniture and tools come from the forest, but also their heat, hunting, sugar from trees, soap from wood ashes, oak bark for tanning hides, dyes for cloth and charcoal for making gunpowder. Our forefathers literally lived from the wealth of the forests and thought of wood as a great asset and symbol of the riches of America.

Our early pioneers were a plain people, most with little schooling, who learned through experience and built by rule of thumb. They built their homes, buildings and bridges with rough hand-split lumber and hand-hewn timbers, each one bearing their sweat and handprints for all time. They developed a dignity in their functional and simple architectural style that is still being used today.

Pioneers learned forest wisdom from the people who greeted them when they arrived on these shores. The pioneer woodsman and carpenter learned their lesson well from the American Indian. They learned to know wood as it stood in the forest. They knew it by smell, how to season it before cutting, where to grow it, when to cut it and how to use each to its best purpose, such as oak for pegs, hickory for hinges, black gum for plow shares, cedar for pails and shingles, chestnut for barrel hoops, and pine for a soft seat, to name a few.

Our forefathers, who were required to have many talents in order to survive had, above all, a reverence for wood.

> *I built those stalls and that shed there; I am barber,*
> *leech and doctor. I am a weaver, a shoemaker, farrier,*
> *wheelwright, farmer, gardener, and when it can't be*
> *helped, a soldier.*
>
> —FROM *Travels in the Confederation, 1783.*

The first bridge was probably built by nomads fleeing danger or seeking an area of more food. We can assume that his "bridge" was a hasty and temporary device made with material at hand—a fallen tree, long flat stones, bamboo or vines. As man settled on land, raising crops and livestock, he realized there would be continuing benefits with a more permanent structure; thus, the art of bridge building began.

History records three basic types of bridges: the *beam* bridge, a tree spanning a river; the *arch,* one we know so well from Roman history; and the *suspension,* originally a vine tied between trees to walk on with another vine tied about four feet higher on the same trees to serve as a hand rail. Heaven help one going across when a strong wind arises and the ropes starting swinging in opposite directions. Then, only the accomplished acrobat could survive! These early bridges were one-way-at-a-time structures. Later, as man formed communities, bridges were erected to accommodate more people, their flocks and, eventually, their vehicles. Bridge construction became a community and government responsibility.

The earliest bridge of record was built over the river Nile by the first king of the Egyptians in the year 2650 B.C.; a floating bridge appears in the records about 500 B.C. Ruins of earlier bridges, about 4000 B.C., exist but do not appear in any written record.

The Romans were exceptional bridge builders. They built stone bridges 160 feet high with 140 foot spans and foundations up to 16 feet below the river bed. Some of these bridges have survived for about 2,000 years. This fact undoubtedly due to the Roman policy of strict accountability for bridge builders; the builders would not be repaid their deposit until the bridge had successfully stood for forty years.

As Rome declined, so did the building of bridges on the European continent. Generally, the bridges that were built during this time were built by the fuedal lords who not only charged a toll to the traveler crossing *over* the bridge, but also, to the river traffic passing *under* the bridge. Later, kings took away the lords' privilege of levying tolls and kept it for themselves.

During the Dark Ages (300-600 A.D.) bridges in France were considered a rare luxury and were frequently fortified to be used in the defense of a city. Some of the bridges contained mini-cities having shops, houses and chapels on either side of the roadway and hosting festivals and tournaments on special days. Congestion on these city-bridges was severe and fires and accidents were common.

Times improved in the early Middle Ages and people started to build bridges again. These were not on the grand Roman scale; they were of the wooden beam variety. As years passed and long lost engineering skills resurfaced, large stone, and stone and timber bridges began reappearing on the landscape.

BRIDGES

In some areas of Europe where wood was plentiful as in Switzerland and northern Italy, wooden bridges flourished and in the fourteenth century the covered wooden bridge made its debut. Some of the boldest covered bridges were built in Switzerland, but the finest development of these bridges took place in America in the early to mid-1800's. The ones that remain today are looked upon as national treasures.

Thousands of these covered bridges were built in America after 1800, beginning in the East and spreading across the land to the Pacific shore. The earliest and most influential covered bridge builders were Yankees (Northeasterners). Timothy Palmer built the first covered bridge in America in 1805. Four others who followed and had designs named after them are Burr, Long, Town and Howe.

Early American bridges were often financed by lottery or were privately funded with building costs recovered by tolls. In the mid-1800s the cost of an average covered bridge varied from $1,000 to $3,000, depending on the size; bridge carpenters were paid 65¢ a day, plus three free meals. Tolls varied and were often changed at will. Charge accounts were commonplace. There were special rates for doctors, clergymen and large families. Itinerant peddlers normally traded wares for tolls and access was free if attending church.

These bridges, often named for the closest town or its Builder/owner, made perfect meeting places when the local church was unavailable. They have been used as blockhouses or drill halls in times of war. Wooden bridges were vulnerable and often fell victim to flood waters. Two hundred bridges were swept away in Vermont in a 48 hour period during the 1927 flood. One bridge was washed away less than 12 hours after being completed!

Once iron bridge parts could be mass produced and shipped across the country, the large timber bridges became a rarity. The days of the "wishing bridge" and the "kissing bridge" where young acrobats played in the spruce rafters, where the musty aroma combined with horse smells and loose boards slapped under the wagon wheels were passing. Those that remain today are found on back roads away from the high speed, leveled hills and valleys, and sterilized interstate highway systems.

We would like to see a revival of the art of wooden bridge building and on the following pages, our humble efforts towards this end are presented. A century ago, wood lost its reputation as a suitable construction material for bridges; after a long period of disfavor, we think wood is beginning to regain its lost dignity.

We know wood will never compete with concrete or steel for large bridges, but now there are new methods of treating timber for better and longer use. The small, light or semi-permanent bridges needed all over the world *could* be made of wood. Some arched like rainbows over small streams; some running from building to building or over roadways and small canyons; or bridges just radiating a quiet beauty and grace in a garden can return to serve us and provide delightful moments and memories.

Cumberland

Length: forty feet.

Width: thirteen feet, ten inches.

Weight capacity: 175 people* (see page 3)

STOP
PAY TOLL

Each foot passenger.	2 cents
Each live head of sheep, calves or hogs.	1 cent
Each neat creature whether led or drove.	6 cents
Each horse, jack, or mule.	6 cents
Each horse or mule and rider.	9 cents
Each two wheel cart, pleasure carriage, stage or wagon drawn by one horse, jack, mule or ox.	13 cents
And 6 cents for each additional drawing animal.	
Each 4 wheel wagon or pleasure carriage drawn by one horse, jack, mule or ox.	16 cents
And 9 cents for each additional drawing animal.	
Each sleigh, sled, freight or Burthen wagon drawn by one horse, mule, jack or ox.	11 cents
And 6 cents for each additional drawing animal.	

NORTH FORK

Length: ten feet. Width: four feet, three inches. Weight capacity: 13 people* (see page 3)

Length: twenty-two feet. Width: six feet. Weight capacity: 40 people (see page 3)*

Hudson

Length: twenty-five feet.

Width: fifteen feet, five inches.

Weight capacity: 120 people * *(see page 3)*

WABASH

Length: twenty feet. Width: seven feet, four inches. Weight capacity: 40 people* (see page 3)

Length: twenty-four feet. Width: four feet, three inches. Weight capacity: 30 people* (see page 3)

RUBICON

Length: twelve feet. Width: four feet, four inches. Weight capacity: 15 people *(see page 3)*

Length: twenty-five feet. Width: nine feet. Weight capacity: 70 people* (see page 3)

Length: twenty feet. Width: eight feet, four inches. Weight capacity: 50 people* (see page 3)

Length: twenty feet. Width: six feet, eight inches. Weight capacity: 40 people* (see page 3)

SACRAMENTO

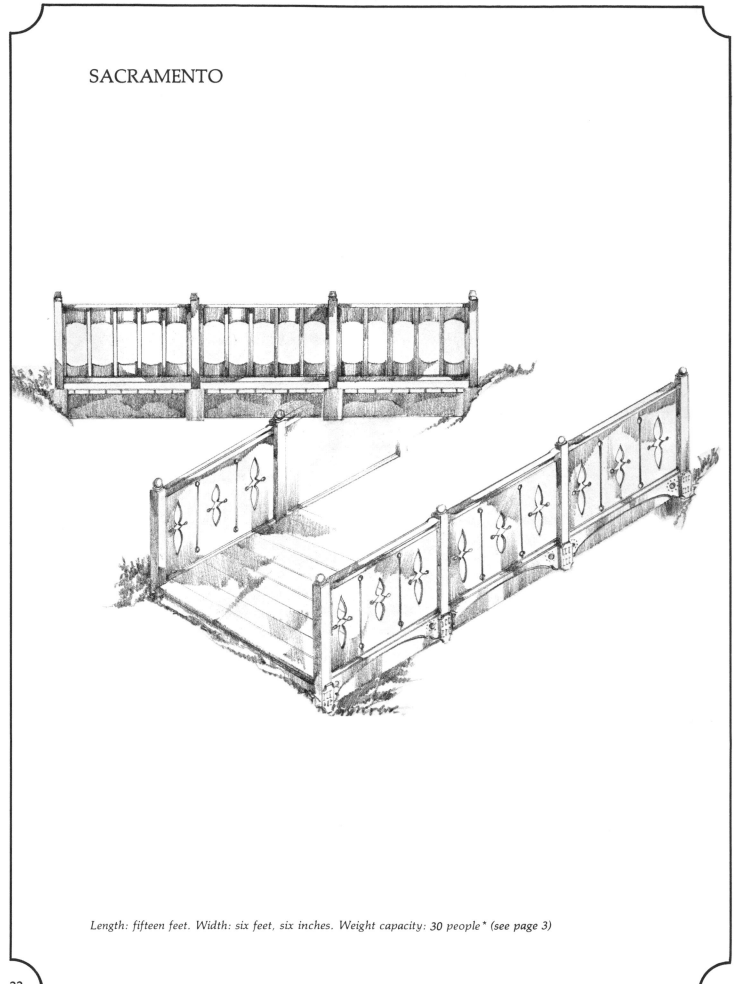

Length: fifteen feet. Width: six feet, six inches. Weight capacity: 30 people **(see page 3)**

Length: fifteen feet. Width: four feet, five inches. Weight capacity: 18 people* (see page 3)

Length: thirty-five feet. Width: ten feet, ten inches. Weight capacity: 120 people (see page 3)*

Length: twenty feet. Width: six feet, eight inches. Weight capacity: 40 people (see page 3)*

Susquehanna

Length: thirty feet.

Width: nine feet, six inches.

Weight capacity: 90 people (see page 3)*

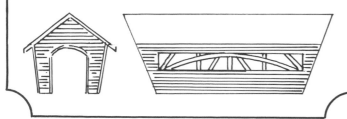

TOLLS

Because no tree was more important than the apple tree, which offered fruit, vinegar for cooking and preserving, apple butter, cider for drink, and wood for special tools, several American states banned the use of applewood for fuel and some toll-takers of the old covered bridges considered it unlucky to take money for apple-laden wagons on their way to the cider press. So it was the custom to have a bucket of fruit ready beside the driver as payment for their way across the bridge.

PLATTE

Length: twelve feet. Width: six feet, six inches. Weight capacity: 22 people * *(see page 3)*

Length: ten feet. Width: six feet, three inches. Weight capacity: 18 people (see page 3)*

BIG SANDY DRAWBRIDGE

Length: fourteen feet, six inches. Width: seven feet. Weight capacity: 30 people* (see page 3)

*Length: twenty feet. Width: six feet, eight inches. Weight capacity: 40 people * (see page 3)*

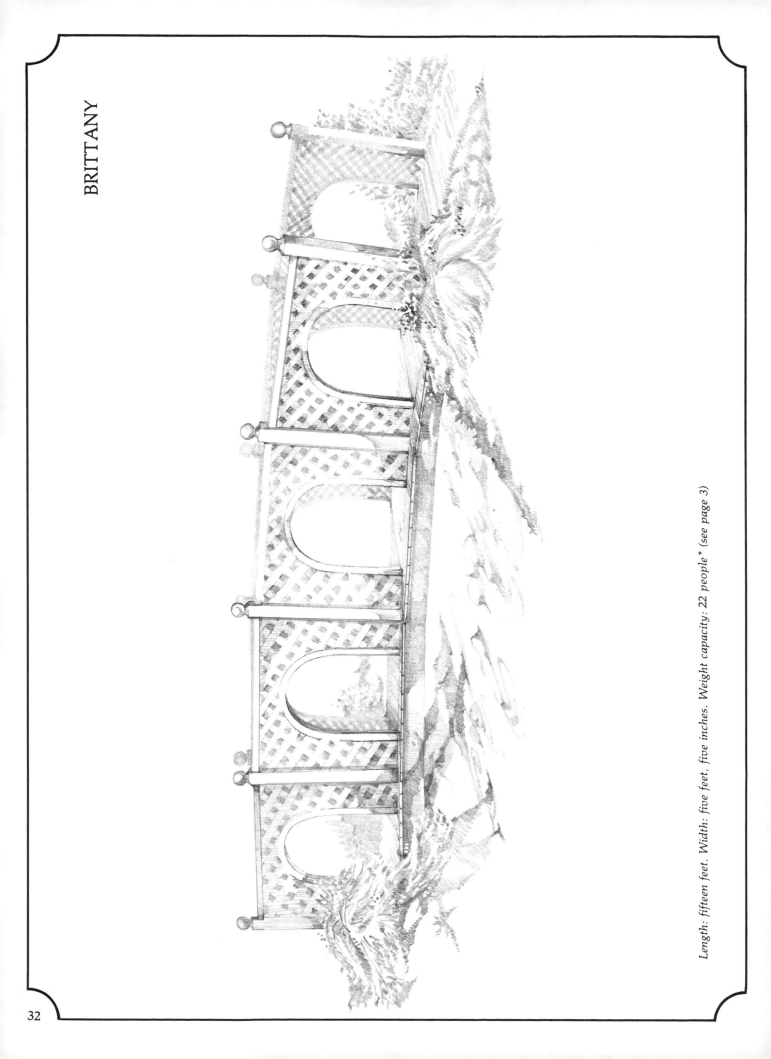

Length: fifteen feet. Width: five feet, five inches. Weight capacity: 22 people * (see page 3)*

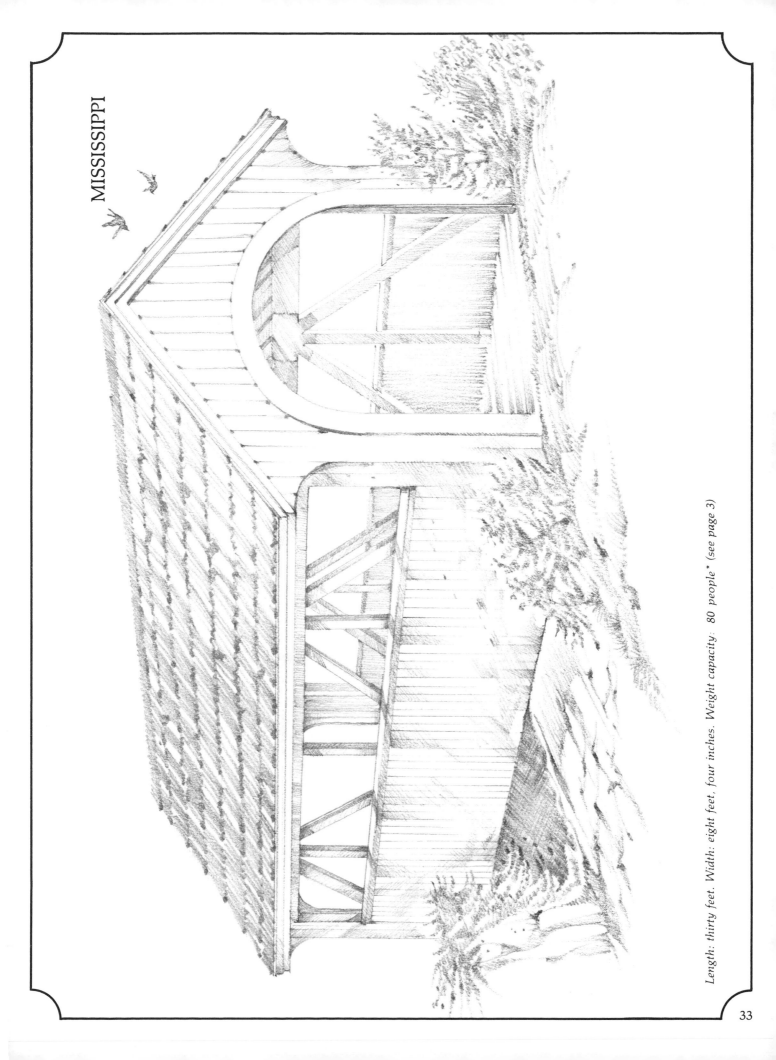

MISSISSIPPI

Length: thirty feet. Width: eight feet, four inches. Weight capacity: 80 people* (see page 3)

33

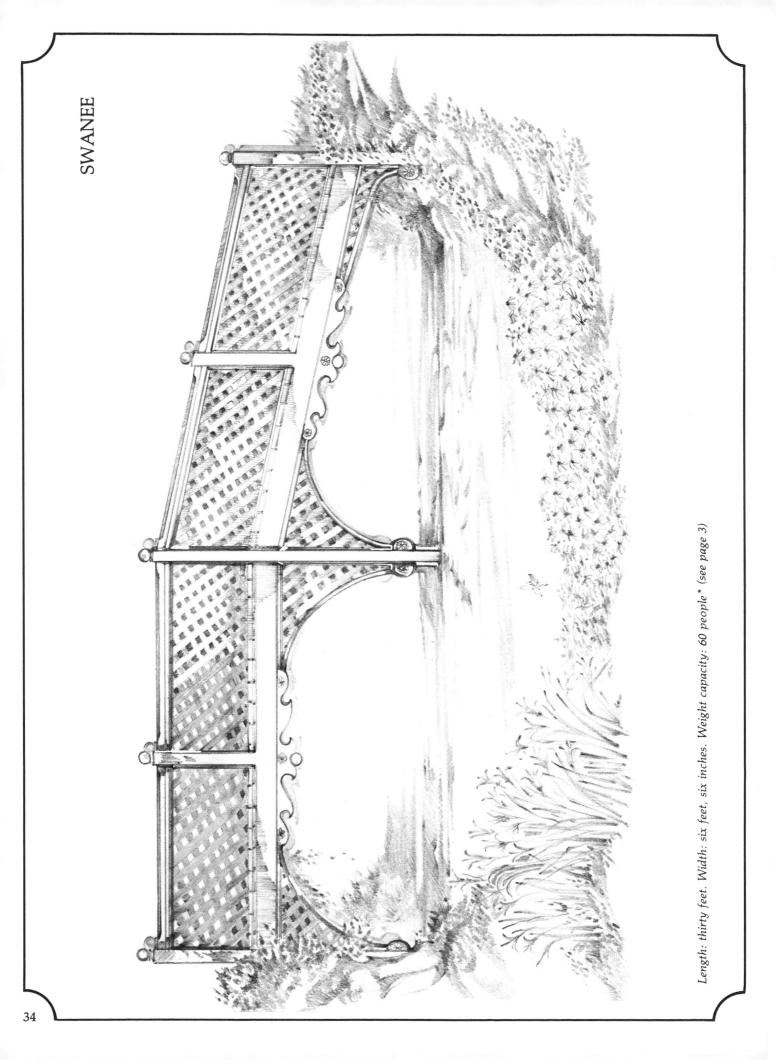

SWANEE

34

*Length: thirty feet. Width: six feet, six inches. Weight capacity: 60 people * (see page 3)*

ROGUE

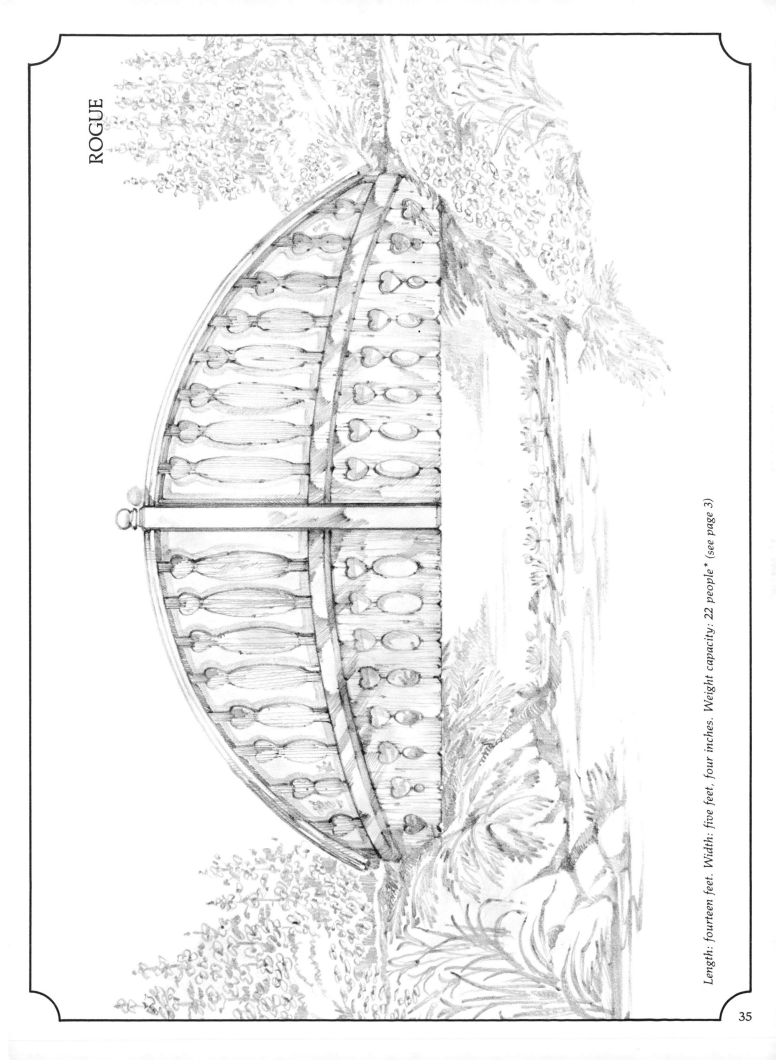

Length: fourteen feet. Width: five feet, four inches. Weight capacity: 22 people* (see page 3)

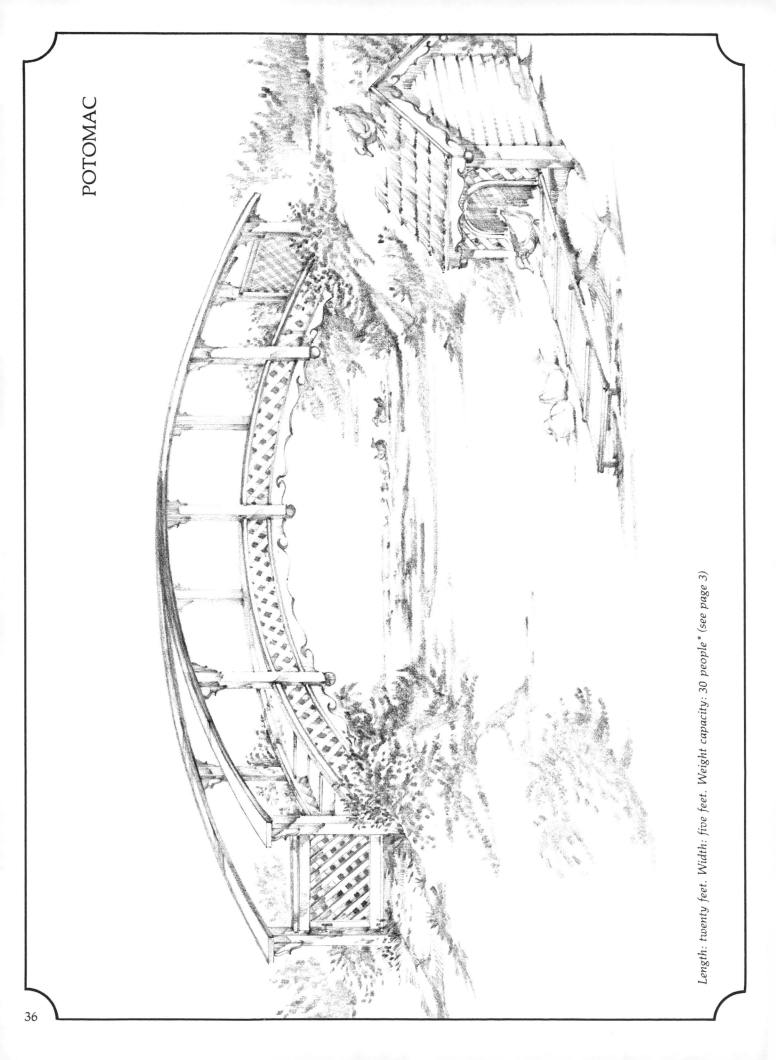

Length: twenty feet. Width: five feet. Weight capacity: 30 people* (see page 3)

COLUMBIA

Length: twenty feet. Width: five feet, three inches. Weight capacity: 33 people* (see page 3)

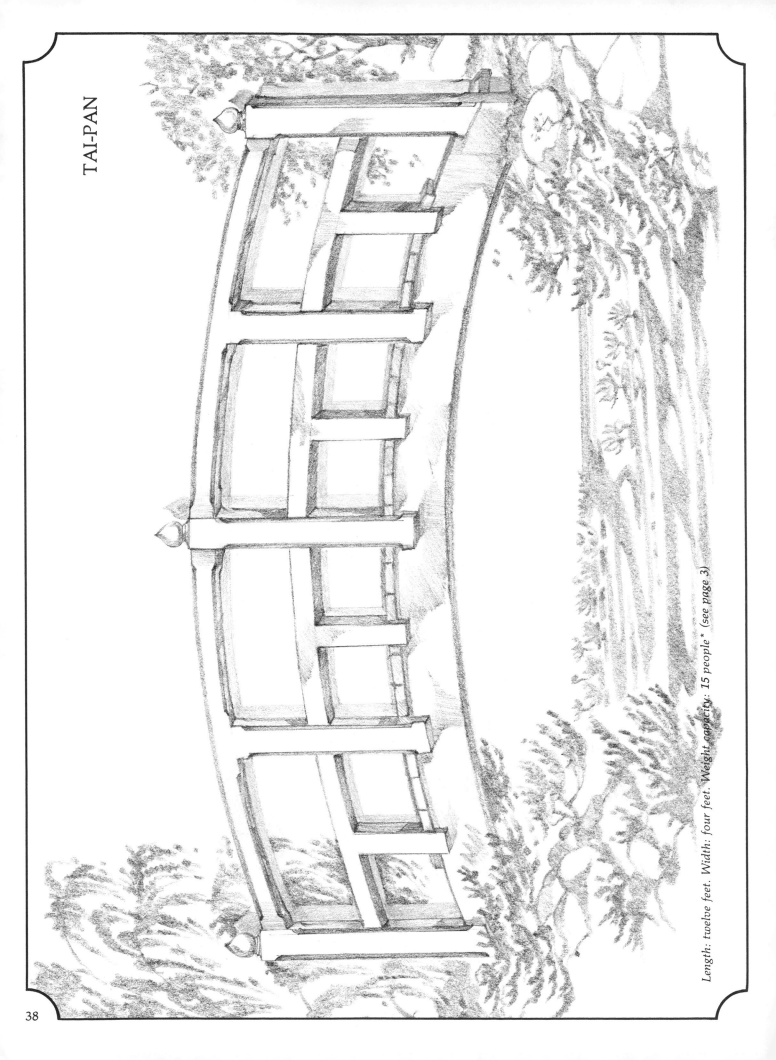

Length: twelve feet. Width: four feet. Weight capacity: 15 people * (see page 3)

SUMIDA

Length: twelve feet. Width: four feet. Weight capacity: 15 people* (see page 3)

Length: twenty-two feet. Width: ten feet, eight inches. Weight capacity: 75 people (see page 3)*

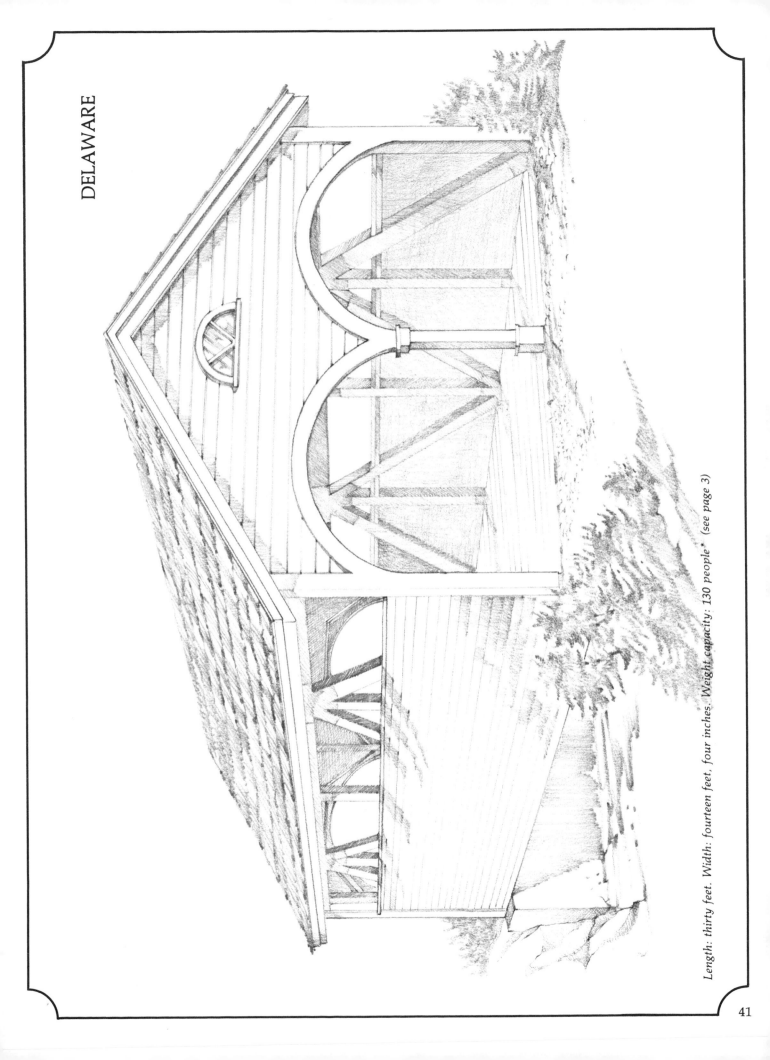

DELAWARE

Length: thirty feet. Width: fourteen feet, four inches. Weight capacity: 130 people* (see page 3)

Cupolas have been serving man for hundreds of years. The name cupola is usually applied to any small turret-like projection on the roof of a building.

In earlier times cupolas would ventilate a building by inducing convection currents that pull cool air from the outside into the bottom of a house, while hot air would exhaust through the top (the chimney effect). Many of America's early God-fearing farmers refused to use lightning rods on their barns as lightning was God's will. They would use cupola ventilators believing that the heat of fresh hay attracted electricity but a good ventilating cupola would repel lightning. Cupolas were used on other buildings and for other purposes, both decorative and functional.

Belvederes are a distinct kind of cupola because they are specifically built for enjoying the view from the roof top of a house, as well as for ventilation. Literally the word *belvedere* derives from the Italian words *bello,* or beautiful, and *vedere,* to see. Thus, a belvedere is a place from which to see beauty.

Belvederes are commonly found on Italianate style houses in America. Highly decorative and popular, they were often put on houses of varied architectural design. They are most often square and large enough to accommodate one or more people.

A common myth says that belvederes were built on sea captains' houses allowing captains to look out and check the weather, or their wives to keep watch for their ships. While this may have been true in some cases, belvederes and cupolas were built all over this country to view hills and countrysides, as well as the ocean. They were considered to be desirable additions to houses even if the view was not spectacular.

A lantern is a cupola that crowns a dome, usually found on a church or public building. Its function is to allow light to penetrate the interior of the dome. Lanterns are circular in shape and small relative to the dome.

Although architectural dictionaries define the cupola as a dome-like projection which is the classical European form, most cupolas on American houses and barns are square or polygonal. The ones that are not belvederes (too small to stand in and look out of) are found everywhere on any style house. There were many ventilating cupolas used in the South for their practical virtues, and on Orson Fowler octagon houses because of the architect's dedication to healthful air circulation.

Whatever the stated purpose for a particular cupola, we believe it is above all decorative. It and its cousin, the bell tower, are closely associated with our American architectural heritage and history. Its design developed into a folk art as each farmer and craftsman chose to express himself by designing an individual styled cupola.

We like cupolas for the character and personality they give to a building. On the following pages we show pen and ink illustrations of thirty-six designs that we like very much. We hope you agree. Do you recognize any?

CUPOLAS

Here are a few old-time Church Bell Codes:

Church bells rang at — 7 A.M.
                     — 12 noon
                     — 9 P.M. (curfew)

Deaths were tolled — 6 bells for a woman
                       9 bells for a man
after a pause, the deceased's age was tolled in bells

Births were tolled after the 7 A.M. tolling

After 9 P.M. (curfew toll) the day of the month in bells
    was rung   (10 bells for the 10th day.)

NEW YORKER

Length: thirty inches square. Height from ridge line: four feet, six inches.

Length: twenty-four inches maximum, point to point. Height from ridge line: two feet, nine inches.

KANSAS

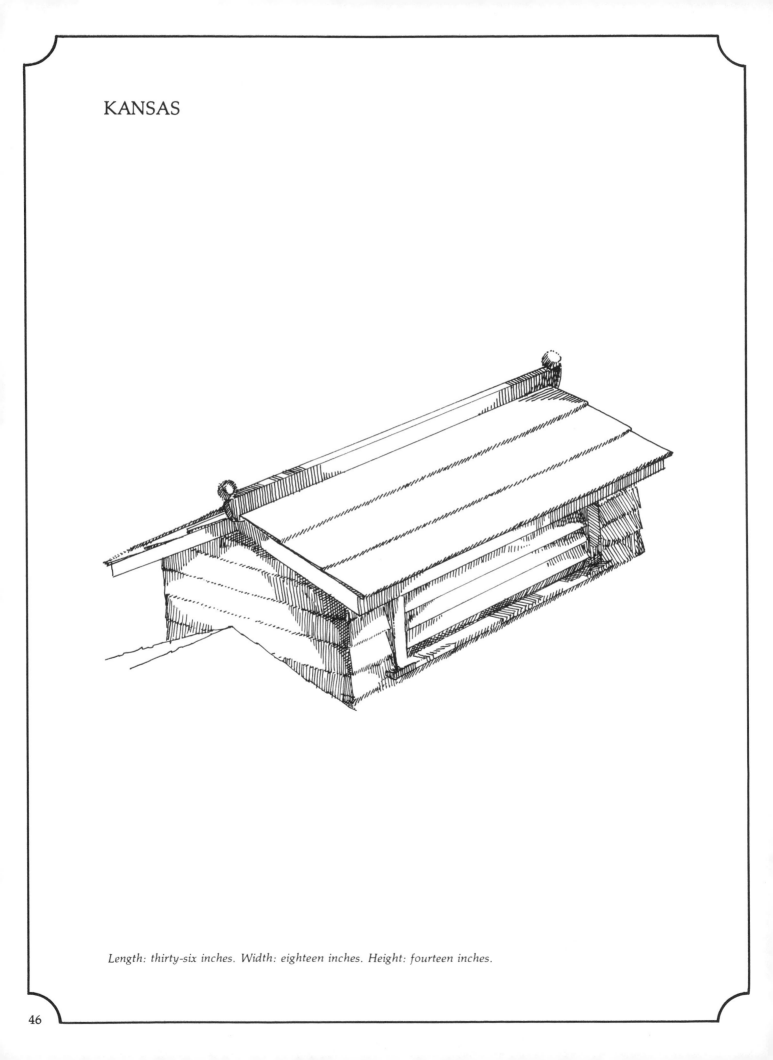

Length: thirty-six inches. Width: eighteen inches. Height: fourteen inches.

Length: two feet, nine inches maximum, point to point. Height from ridge line: four feet, six inches.

LENINGRAD

Length: twenty-four inches diameter. Height from ridge line: four feet, two inches.

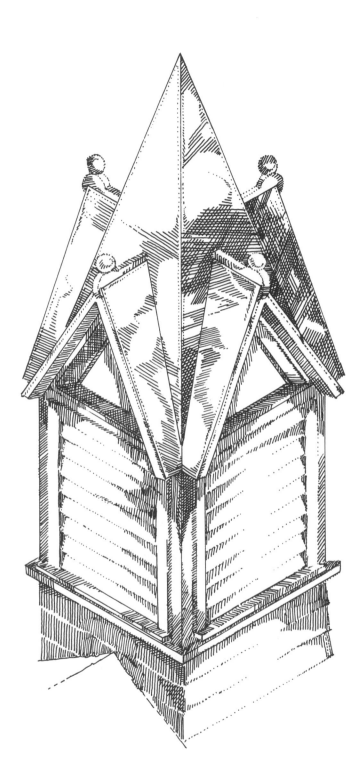

Length: eighteen inches square. Height from ridge line: four feet, ten inches.

WYOMING

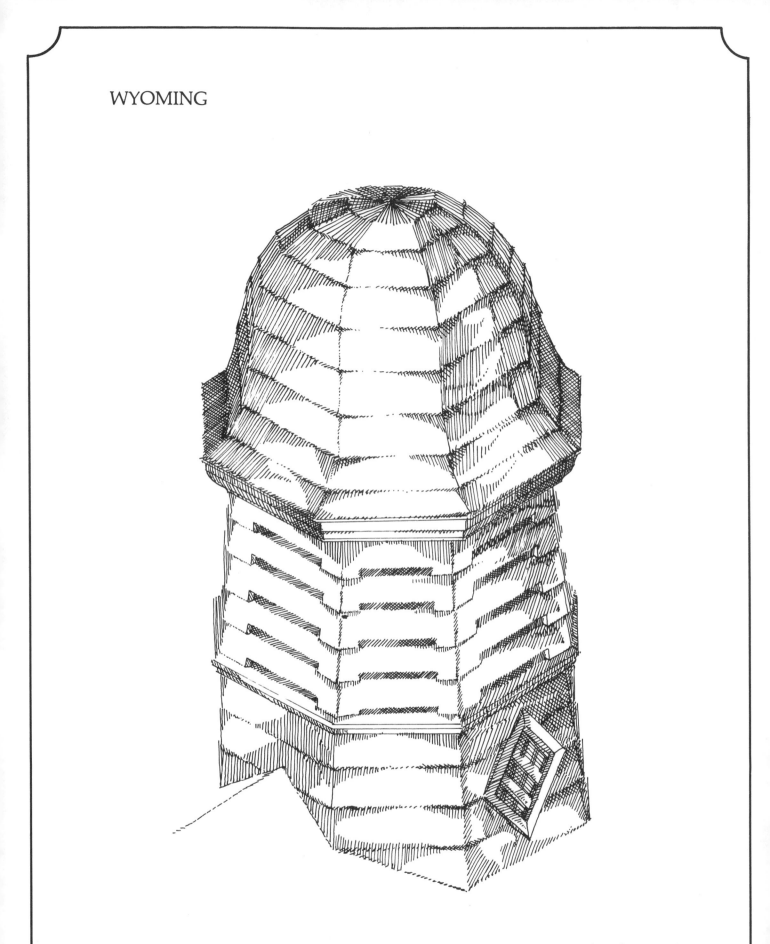

Length: twenty-four inches maximum, point to point. Height from ridge line: three feet, eight inches.

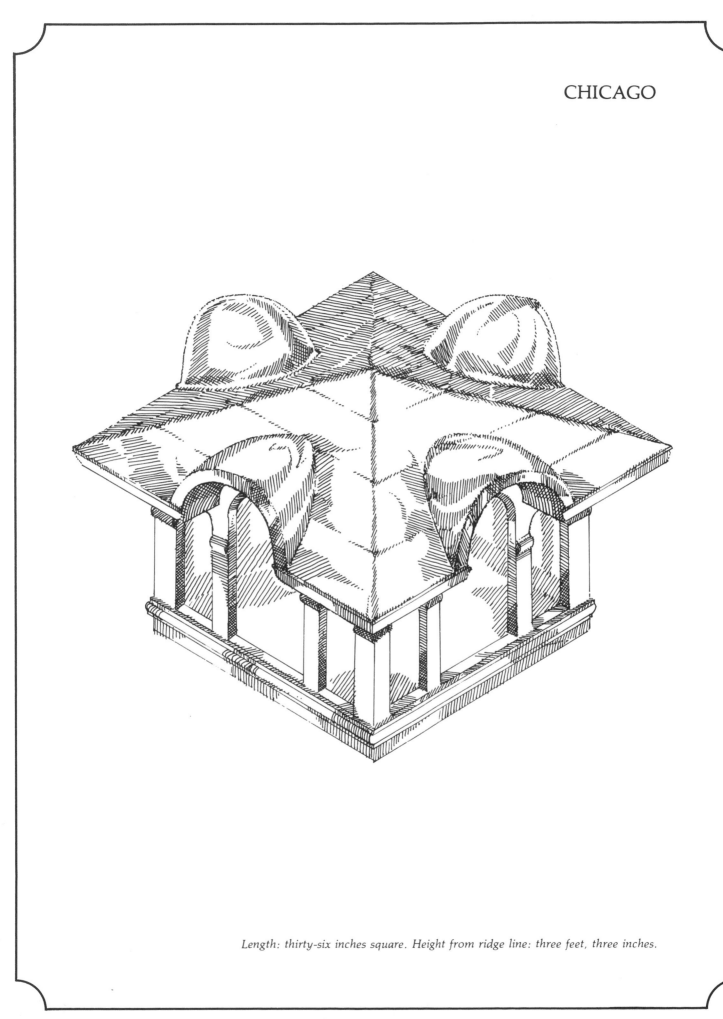

Length: thirty-six inches square. Height from ridge line: three feet, three inches.

HAMPSHIRE

Length: eighteen inches square. Height from ridge line: two feet, five inches.

Length: thirty inches square. Height from ridge line: three feet, nine inches.

Length: twenty-four inches square. Height from ridge line: four feet, two inches.

Length: two feet, eleven inches maximum, point to point. Height from ridge line: two feet, five inches, without ironwork.

SEATTLE

Length: thirty inches square. Height from ridge line: four feet, four inches.

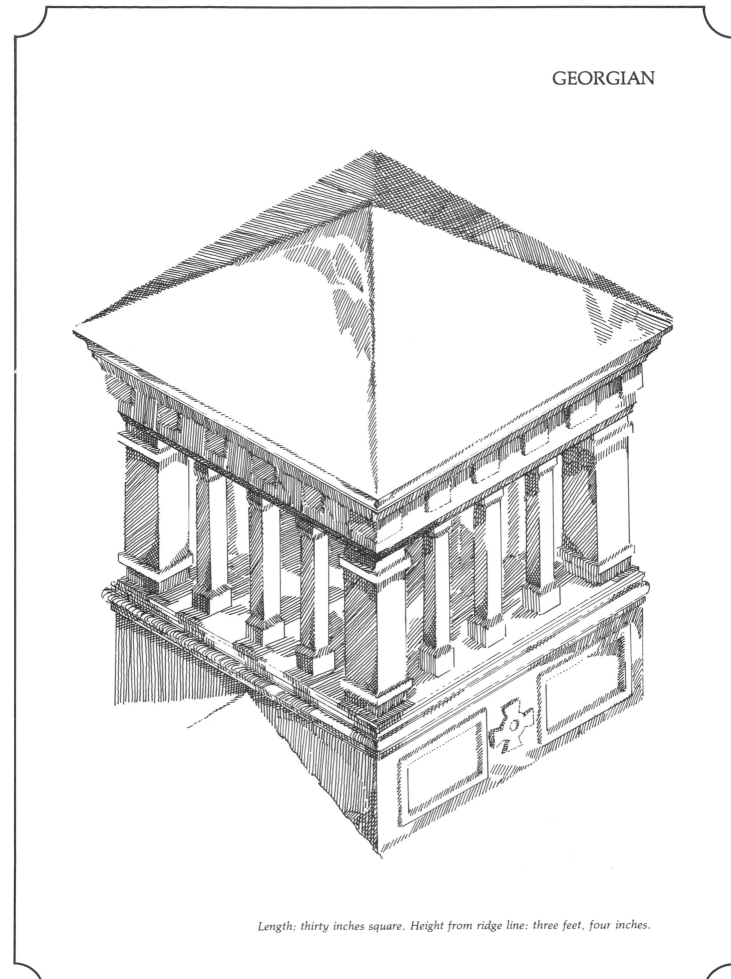

Length: thirty inches square. Height from ridge line: three feet, four inches.

Telemark

Length: thirty-six inches square.
Height from ridge line: five feet, three inches.

McKinnon

Carolina

Length: two feet, nine inches maximum, side to side. Height from ridge line: four feet, one inch.

CAPISTRANO

Length: two feet, four inches maximum, point to point. Height from ridge line: two feet, ten inches.

Length: twenty-one inches square. Height from ridge line: two feet, five inches.

Length: thirty-six inches square. Height from ridge line: five feet, one inch.

Length: forty-eight inches square. Height from ridge line: five feet, one inch.

Length: thirty-six inches square. Height from ridge line: four feet, eight inches.

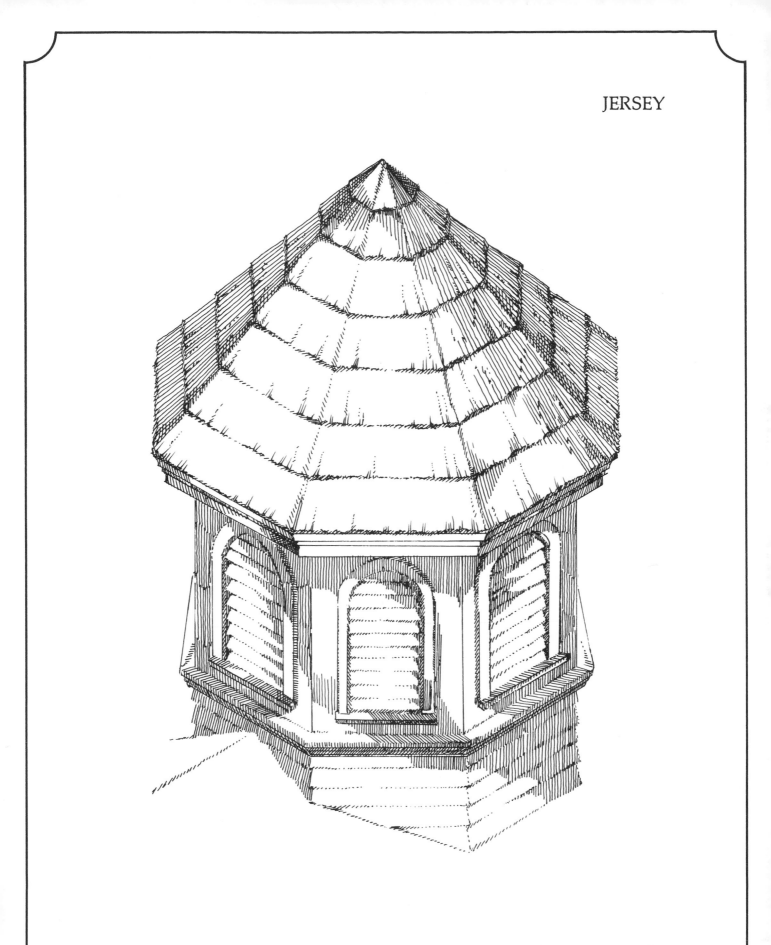

Length: three feet, ten inches maximum, point to point. Height from ridge line: five feet, six inches.

DAKOTA

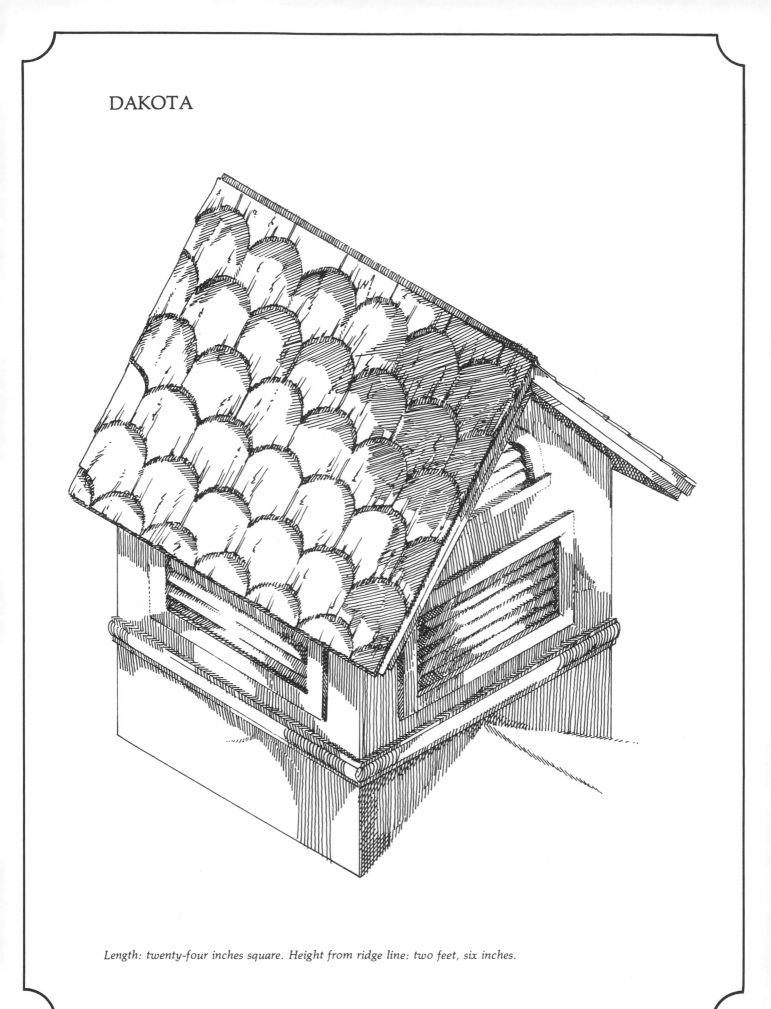

Length: twenty-four inches square. Height from ridge line: two feet, six inches.

Length: forty-eight inches square. Height from ridge line: eight feet, ten inches.

BROOKLYN

Length: eighteen inches square. Height from ridge line: two feet, seven inches.

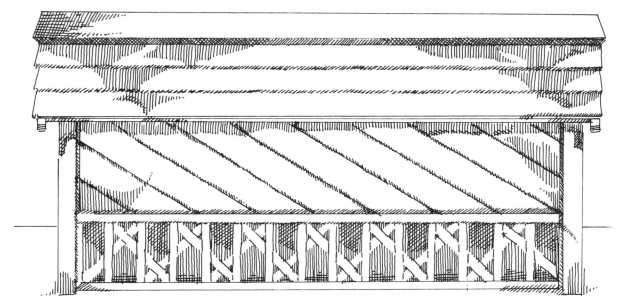

Length: forty-two inches. Width: eighteen inches. Height from ridge line: eighteen inches.

Length: thirty-two inches square. Height from ridge line: six feet, eight inches.

Length: thirty inches square. Height from ridge line: four feet, seven inches.

VERMONT

Length: twenty-eight inches square. Height from ridge line: four feet, ten inches.

Length: twenty-eight inches square. Height from ridge line: three feet, three inches.

Length: twenty-four inches square. Height from ridge line: two feet, eight inches.

Length: forty inches square. Height from ridge line: six feet, ten inches.

Length: forty-eight inches square. Height from ridge line: seven feet, three inches.

Length: twenty-two inches square. Height from ridge line: three feet.

ALBERTA

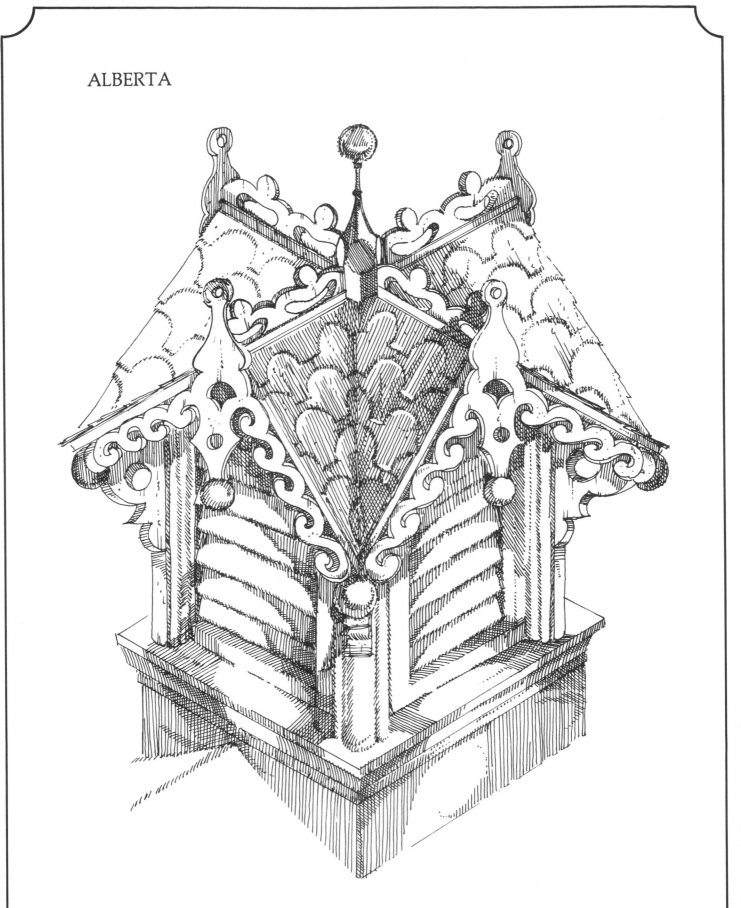

Length: thirty-four inches square.
Height from ridge line: four feet, eight inches.

Length: twenty-eight inches square.
Height from ridge line: two feet, eight inches.

BRIDGE PLANS

GENERAL INFORMATION FOR BRIDGE CONSTRUCTION AND DESIGN NOTES

We believe these general recommendations to be good advice and should be followed when building a bridge from our plans. Restrict bridge traffic to people, bicycles, and small garden tractors.

To begin with, contact should be made with your local units of government to inquire about State and local building regulations and permits regarding bridges. If there is a difference between these plans and local regulations, the local regulations should be followed in all cases.

The bridge foundations are designed not to exceed 12' from footing to top of foundation and to be used in soil that has been tested to have a minimum bearing of 1500 pounds per square foot. If these specifications are changed or if the span or width of the bridge, or any structurally integral component is to be changed or altered, consult with a qualified registered structural engineer. This also applies to loads (weights) imposed when larger than that indicated as the "design load" on the bridge design specifications. Also, no deviations from the foundation and foundation footings size, shape, and reinforcing steel shall be made.

Douglas Fir or Hem-Fir structural grade #1 (minimum Fb = 1400 strength) should be used for all structural members such as beams, posts, gables, headers, decking and rafters. Use clear pine (best knotless grade available) for trim fascias, and railing (Fir or cedar may be substituted.) The wood dimensions given are nominal (not actual.) For example: a $2'' \times 4''$'s actual dimensions are $1^1/_2'' \times 3^1/_2''$. Bolts and connection steel plate should conform to the steel industry's best standards, and be high strength and atmospheric corrosion-resistant.

It is important to use good construction practices such as temporary bracing, square, straight and true foundation lines, and a transit for correct leveling and heights. All work should be done in a workmanlike manner and care should be taken to see that all parts are properly nailed, fastened, welded or fitted. Double check all your measurements before you do any cutting and consult an experienced carpenter or bridge builder if necessary. All welding should be done by a certified and experienced welder.

All outdoor wood structures are subject to varying weather conditions. To prolong their life, it is advisable to use good quality pressure-treated wood components throughout. If by chance you have various trim pieces not pressure-treated, apply a preservative such as pentachlorophenol to retard deterioration.

ROGUE

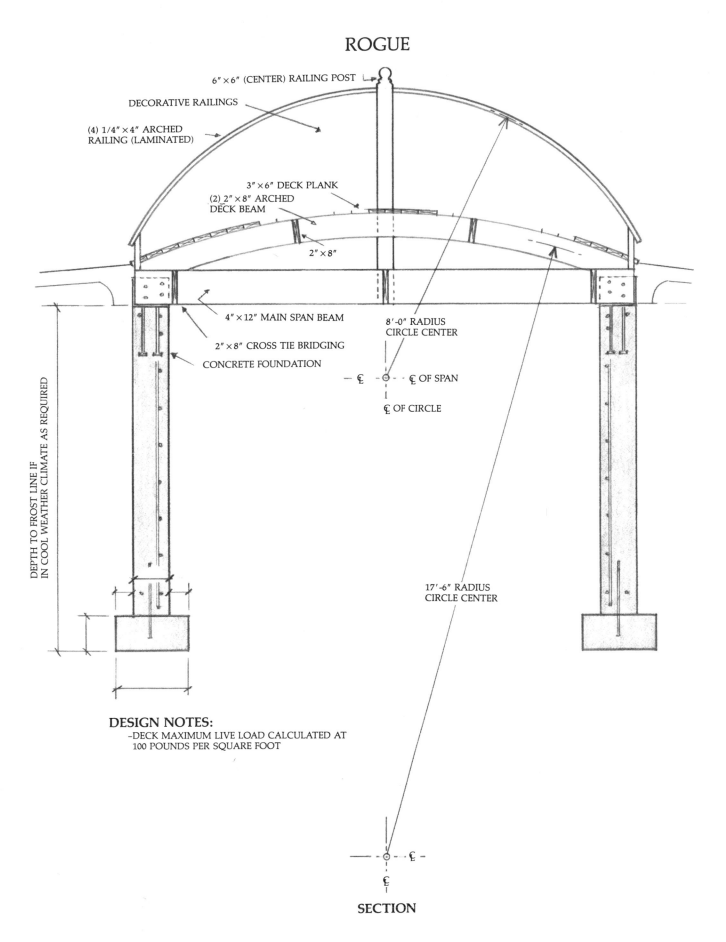

6″ × 6″ (CENTER) RAILING POST

DECORATIVE RAILINGS

(4) 1/4″ × 4″ ARCHED
RAILING (LAMINATED)

3″ × 6″ DECK PLANK

(2) 2″ × 8″ ARCHED
DECK BEAM

2″ × 8″

4″ × 12″ MAIN SPAN BEAM

8′-0″ RADIUS
CIRCLE CENTER

2″ × 8″ CROSS TIE BRIDGING

CONCRETE FOUNDATION

DEPTH TO FROST LINE IF
IN COOL WEATHER CLIMATE AS REQUIRED

℄ ℄ OF SPAN

℄ OF CIRCLE

17′-6″ RADIUS
CIRCLE CENTER

DESIGN NOTES:
–DECK MAXIMUM LIVE LOAD CALCULATED AT
100 POUNDS PER SQUARE FOOT

℄

℄

SECTION

ROGUE

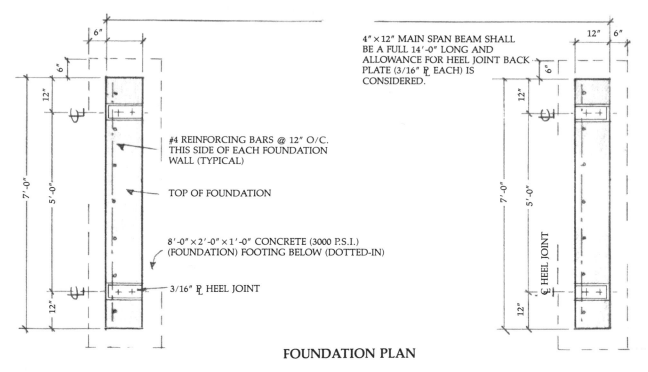

4" × 12" MAIN SPAN BEAM SHALL BE A FULL 14'-0" LONG AND ALLOWANCE FOR HEEL JOINT BACK PLATE (3/16" ℞ EACH) IS CONSIDERED.

#4 REINFORCING BARS @ 12" O/C. THIS SIDE OF EACH FOUNDATION WALL (TYPICAL)

TOP OF FOUNDATION

8'-0" × 2'-0" × 1'-0" CONCRETE (3000 P.S.I.) (FOUNDATION) FOOTING BELOW (DOTTED-IN)

3/16" ℞ HEEL JOINT

FOUNDATION PLAN

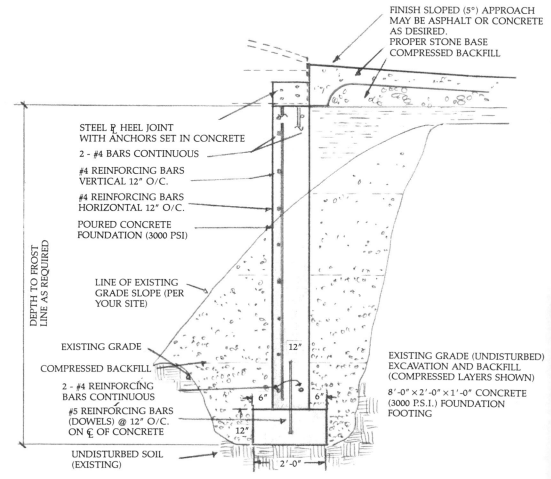

FINISH SLOPED (5°) APPROACH MAY BE ASPHALT OR CONCRETE AS DESIRED. PROPER STONE BASE COMPRESSED BACKFILL

STEEL ℞ HEEL JOINT WITH ANCHORS SET IN CONCRETE

2 - #4 BARS CONTINUOUS

#4 REINFORCING BARS VERTICAL 12" O/C.

#4 REINFORCING BARS HORIZONTAL 12" O/C.

POURED CONCRETE FOUNDATION (3000 PSI)

LINE OF EXISTING GRADE SLOPE (PER YOUR SITE)

EXISTING GRADE

COMPRESSED BACKFILL

2 - #4 REINFORCING BARS CONTINUOUS

#5 REINFORCING BARS (DOWELS) @ 12" O/C. ON ℞ OF CONCRETE

UNDISTURBED SOIL (EXISTING)

DEPTH TO FROST LINE AS REQUIRED

EXISTING GRADE (UNDISTURBED) EXCAVATION AND BACKFILL (COMPRESSED LAYERS SHOWN)

8'-0" × 2'-0" × 1'-0" CONCRETE (3000 P.S.I.) FOUNDATION FOOTING

FOUNDATION SECTION

ROGUE

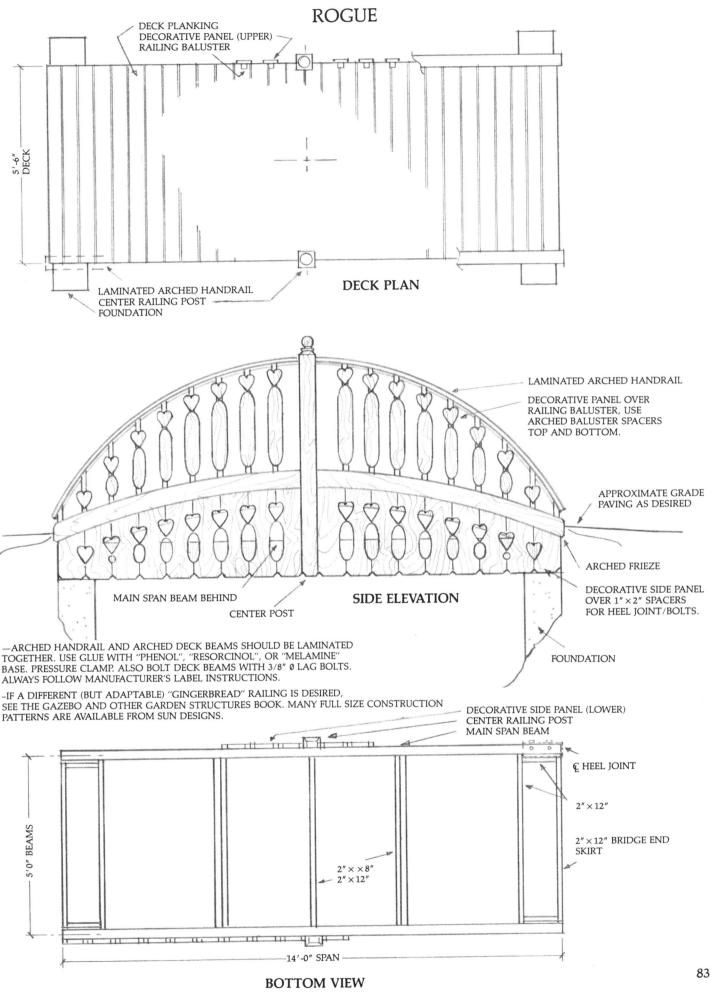

DECK PLANKING
DECORATIVE PANEL (UPPER)
RAILING BALUSTER

5'-6" DECK

LAMINATED ARCHED HANDRAIL
CENTER RAILING POST
FOUNDATION

DECK PLAN

LAMINATED ARCHED HANDRAIL

DECORATIVE PANEL OVER
RAILING BALUSTER, USE
ARCHED BALUSTER SPACERS
TOP AND BOTTOM.

APPROXIMATE GRADE
PAVING AS DESIRED

ARCHED FRIEZE

DECORATIVE SIDE PANEL
OVER 1" × 2" SPACERS
FOR HEEL JOINT/BOLTS.

FOUNDATION

MAIN SPAN BEAM BEHIND

CENTER POST

SIDE ELEVATION

—ARCHED HANDRAIL AND ARCHED DECK BEAMS SHOULD BE LAMINATED
TOGETHER. USE GLUE WITH "PHENOL", "RESORCINOL", OR "MELAMINE"
BASE. PRESSURE CLAMP. ALSO BOLT DECK BEAMS WITH 3/8" Ø LAG BOLTS.
ALWAYS FOLLOW MANUFACTURER'S LABEL INSTRUCTIONS.

–IF A DIFFERENT (BUT ADAPTABLE) "GINGERBREAD" RAILING IS DESIRED,
SEE THE GAZEBO AND OTHER GARDEN STRUCTURES BOOK. MANY FULL SIZE CONSTRUCTION
PATTERNS ARE AVAILABLE FROM SUN DESIGNS.

DECORATIVE SIDE PANEL (LOWER)
CENTER RAILING POST
MAIN SPAN BEAM

₵ HEEL JOINT

2" × 12"

2" × 12" BRIDGE END
SKIRT

5'0" BEAMS

2" × × 8"
2" × 12"

14'-0" SPAN

BOTTOM VIEW

ROGUE

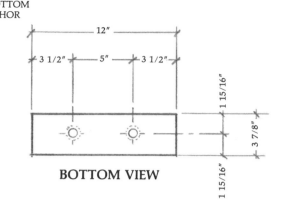

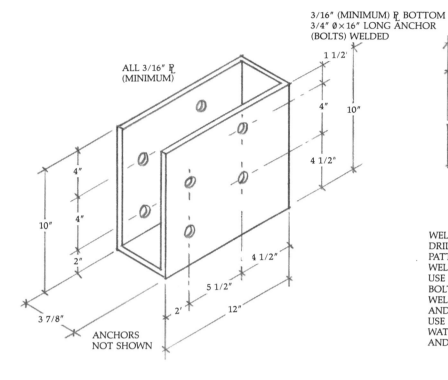

3/16" (MINIMUM) ℞ BOTTOM
3/4" Ø × 16" LONG ANCHOR
(BOLTS) WELDED

ALL 3/16" ℞
(MINIMUM)

1 1/2'

4"

10"

4 1/2"

4"

10"

4"

2"

4 1/2"

5 1/2"

3 7/8"

2'

12"

ANCHORS
NOT SHOWN

12"

3 1/2"   5"   3 1/2"

1 15/16"

3 7/8"

1 15/16"

BOTTOM VIEW

WELD 4-℞ PIECES TOGETHER. CORNERS SQUARE.
DRILL 13/16" Ø HOLES THRU IN IDENTICAL
PATTERN AS SHOWN
WELD BOTTOM ANCHORS.
USE STEEL INDUSTRY BEST STANDARD ℞,
BOLTS, AND WELDING.
WELDING SHALL BE DONE BY A QUALIFIED
AND EXPERIENCED WELDER.
USE 3/4" Ø BOLTS WITH 1 1/2" WASHERS.
WATER/WEATHER PROOF ALL BOLT, NUT,
AND WASHER, AND ℞ SURFACES.

HEEL JOINT

ROGUE
BRIDGE MATERIAL LIST

ITEM	NUMBER	DESCRIPTION
1		CONCRETE FOUNDATION AND FOOTING (3000 P.S.I.) READY MIX
2		STEEL REINFORCING BARS GRADE 60
3	4 PCS	STEEL PLATE HEEL JOINTS WITH ANCHORS WELDED (3/16" WELDED ℞)
4	16 PCS	3/4"Ø×4 1/2" LONG BOLTS (BEAMS)
5	10 PCS	STOCK STEEL JOIST HANGERS (FLOOR TIES)
6	6 PCS	3/8"Ø×8" LONG BOLTS (POSTS)
7	24 PCS	3"×6" S4S FIR PLAN DECKING (6')
8	3 PCS	2"×12" S4S FIR FLOOR CROSS TIE BRIDGING (5')
9	2 PCS	2"×8" S4S FIR FLOOR CROSS TIE BRIDGING (5')
10	2 PCS	4"×12" S4S FIR MAIN SPAN BEAM
11	6 PCS	2"×12" S4S FIR DECK BRIDGE END SKIRT (5',1')
12	2 PCS	1/4" CDX PLYWOOD DECK BRIDGE END SKIRT PAD (5'×1')
13	8 PCS	2"×8" S4S FIR ARCHED DECK SPAN BEAMS (ARCHED CUT)
14	88 LF	1"×6" S4S PINE/FIR DECORATIVE SIDE PANEL (TOP)
15	78 LF	1"×10" S4S PINE/FIR DECORATIVE SIDE PANEL (BOTTOM)
16	2 PCS	6"×6" SRS PINE/FIR RAILING POSTS (7')
17	136 LF	1/4"×4" S4S FIR RAILING CAP (LAMINATED)
18	29 LF	1"×12" S4S PINE/FIR FRIEZE (ARCHED CUT)
19	2 LF	3/8" Ø HARDWOOD DOWEL (RAILING CONNECTIONS)
20	95 LF	1"×2" S4S PINE/FIR BALUSTER AND RAILING SPACERS (ARCHED CUT AND STRAIGHT)
21	84 LF	2"×2" S4S PINE/FIR BALUSTER
22		STEEL LAG BOLTS AS REQUIRED
23		6D, 8D, 10D, 16D NAILS AS REQUIRED

THIS MATERIAL LIST IS PROVIDED TO ASSIST YOU IN THE PROCUREMENT OF NECESSARY ITEMS FROM
YOUR LOCAL LUMBER YARD. YOU MAY FIND IT NECESSARY TO OBTAIN MORE OF CERTAIN ITEMS DUE
TO CONSTRUCTION WASTE, ETC.

ROGUE

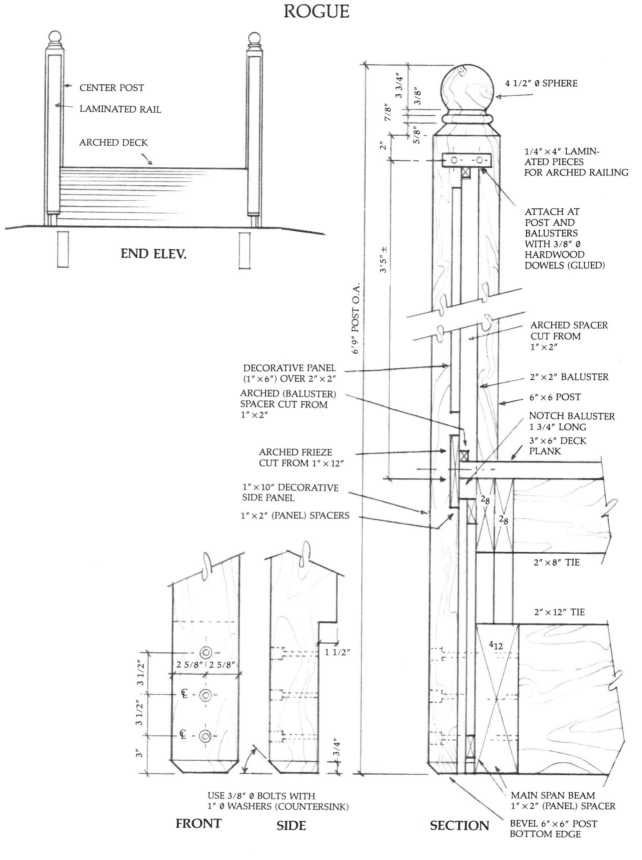

END ELEV.

CENTER POST

LAMINATED RAIL

ARCHED DECK

4 1/2" Ø SPHERE

3 3/4"
3/8"
7/8"
5/8"
2"

1/4" × 4" LAMIN-
ATED PIECES
FOR ARCHED RAILING

ATTACH AT
POST AND
BALUSTERS
WITH 3/8" Ø
HARDWOOD
DOWELS (GLUED)

6'9" POST O.A.

3'5" ±

ARCHED SPACER
CUT FROM
1" × 2"

2" × 2" BALUSTER

6" × 6 POST

NOTCH BALUSTER
1 3/4" LONG

3" × 6" DECK
PLANK

DECORATIVE PANEL
(1" × 6") OVER 2" × 2"

ARCHED (BALUSTER)
SPACER CUT FROM
1" × 2"

ARCHED FRIEZE
CUT FROM 1" × 12"

1" × 10" DECORATIVE
SIDE PANEL

1" × 2" (PANEL) SPACERS

2_8

2_8

2" × 8" TIE

2" × 12" TIE

4_{12}

2 5/8" 2 5/8"

3 1/2"

3 1/2"

3 1/2"

3"

1 1/2"

3/4"

USE 3/8" Ø BOLTS WITH
1" Ø WASHERS (COUNTERSINK)

FRONT   **SIDE**   **SECTION**

MAIN SPAN BEAM
1" × 2" (PANEL) SPACER

BEVEL 6" × 6" POST
BOTTOM EDGE

POST DETAIL

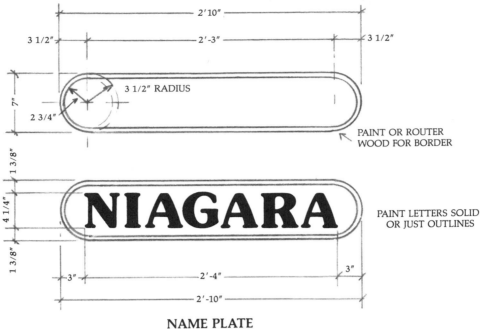

PAINT OR ROUTER
WOOD FOR BORDER

PAINT LETTERS SOLID
OR JUST OUTLINES

NAME PLATE
NO SCALE

NIAGARA BRIDGE MATERIAL LIST

ITEM	NUMBER	DESCRIPTION
1		CONCRETE-FOUNDATION AND FOOTING (3000 P.S.I.) READY MIX
2		STEEL REINFORCING BARS GRADE 60
3	4 PCS	STEEL PLATE HEEL JOINTS WITH ANCHORS WELDED (3/16" WELDED ℞)
4	22 PCS	STEEL PLATE (TRUSS) CONNECTION (3/16" ℞)
5	156 PCS	3/4" Ø × 4 1/2" LONG BOLTS
6	34 PCS	STOCK STEEL RAFTER TIES TO PLATE
7	8 PCS	4" × 10" S4S FIR TRUSS BOTTOM CHORD (10' IF SPLICED)
8	4 PCS	4" × 6" S4S FIR TRUSS WEBB (10')
9	6 PCS	4" × 6" S4S FIR TRUSS TOP CHORD (5', 10' IF SPLICED)
10	10 PCS	4" × 4" S4S FIR TRUSS WEBB (10', 9')
11	7 PCS	2" × 12" S4S FIR DECK-PURLIN HEADERS AND DIAGONAL BRACING (8', 2')
12	6 PCS	2" × 12" S4S FIR DECK BRIDGE AND SKIRT (8', 2')
13	2 PCS	1/4" CDX PLYWOOD DECK BRIDGE END SKIRT PAD (8' × 1')
14	34 PCS	4" × 8" S4S FIR DECK PLANKING (8'-3 1/2")
15	34 PCS	2" × 6" S4S FIR RAFTERS (6'-6", 5'-4")
16	17 PCS	2" × 6" S4S FIR CEILING CROSS TIE (8'-3 1/2")
17	17 PCS	1" × 6" S4S FIR COLLAR TIE (4'-6")
18	26 LF	1" × 2" RED CEDAR FINISH FASCIA TRIM RAKE
19	21 LF	2" × 8" S4S FIR RIDGE BRD
20	70 LF	2" × 4" S4S FIR GABLE ENDS BLOCKING, BRACING, & DOOR BRACING
21	510 LF	1" × 8" S4S CEDAR TONGUE AND GROOVE V-JOINT SIDEING
22	4 SHTS	1" CDX PLYWOOD ENDWALL SHEATHING
23	50 LF	1" × 6" RED CEDAR OPENING (DOORWAY) TRIM
24	6 LF	1" × 8" RED CEDAR OPENING TOP NAME PLATE
25	39 LF	2" × 6" RED CEDAR OPENING RETURN TRIM CAP
26	23 LF	1" × 4" RED CEDAR DOORWAY RETURN TRIM
27	7 SHTS	3/4" CDX PLYWOOD SIDEWALL SHEATHING
28	35 LF	2" × 4" S4S FIR WALL OPENING CAP HEADER
29	2.7 SQ	HAND SPLIT RED CEDAR SHAKES
30	273 SF	43 LB. DBLE. COATED TAR FELT
31	13 SHTS	1/2" CDX PLYWOOD ROOF SHEATHING-OPTION
32	460 LF	1" × 8" S4S PINE/FIR ROOF DECK-OPTION
33		STEEL LAG BOLTS AS REQUIRED
34		6D, 8D, 16D, AND ROOFING NAILS AS REQUIRED

THIS MATERIAL LIST IS PROVIDED TO ASSIST YOU IN THE PROCUREMENT OF NECESSARY ITEMS FROM YOUR LOCAL LUMBER YARD. YOU MAY FIND IT NECESSARY TO OBTAIN MORE OF CERTAIN ITEMS DUE TO CONSTRUCTION WASTE, ETC.

NIAGARA

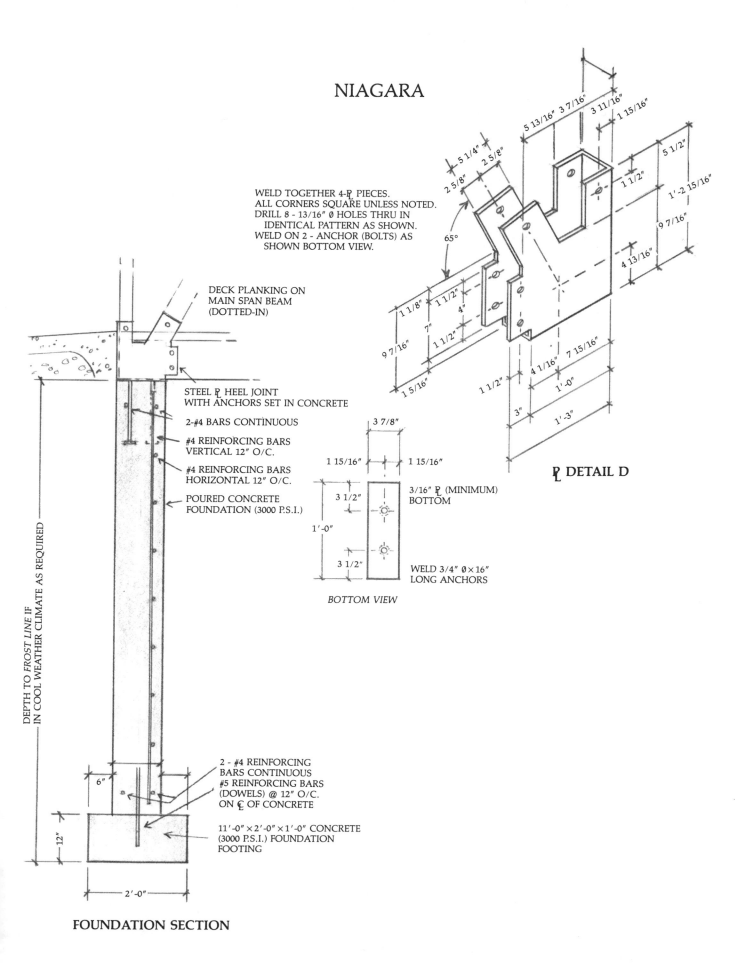

WELD TOGETHER 4-℞ PIECES.
ALL CORNERS SQUARE UNLESS NOTED.
DRILL 8 - 13/16″ Ø HOLES THRU IN
IDENTICAL PATTERN AS SHOWN.
WELD ON 2 - ANCHOR (BOLTS) AS
SHOWN BOTTOM VIEW.

5 13/16″ 3 7/16″
3 11/16″
1 15/16″
5 1/4″
2 5/8″
2 5/8″
5 1/2″
1 1/2″
1′-2 15/16″
9 7/16″
65°
4 13/16″
1 1/8″
1 1/2″
4″
9 7/16″
7″
1 1/2″
4 1/16″ 7 15/16″
1 5/16″
1 1/2″
1′-0″
3″
1′-3″

℞ DETAIL D

DECK PLANKING ON
MAIN SPAN BEAM
(DOTTED-IN)

STEEL ℞ HEEL JOINT
WITH ANCHORS SET IN CONCRETE

2-#4 BARS CONTINUOUS

#4 REINFORCING BARS
VERTICAL 12″ O/C.

#4 REINFORCING BARS
HORIZONTAL 12″ O/C.

POURED CONCRETE
FOUNDATION (3000 P.S.I.)

3 7/8″
1 15/16″   1 15/16″
3 1/2″
1′-0″
3 1/2″

3/16″ ℞ (MINIMUM)
BOTTOM

WELD 3/4″ Ø × 16″
LONG ANCHORS

BOTTOM VIEW

DEPTH TO *FROST LINE* IF
IN COOL WEATHER CLIMATE AS REQUIRED

6″

2 - #4 REINFORCING
BARS CONTINUOUS
#5 REINFORCING BARS
(DOWELS) @ 12″ O/C.
ON ℄ OF CONCRETE

11′-0″ × 2′-0″ × 1′-0″ CONCRETE
(3000 P.S.I.) FOUNDATION
FOOTING

12″

2′-0″

FOUNDATION SECTION

NIAGARA

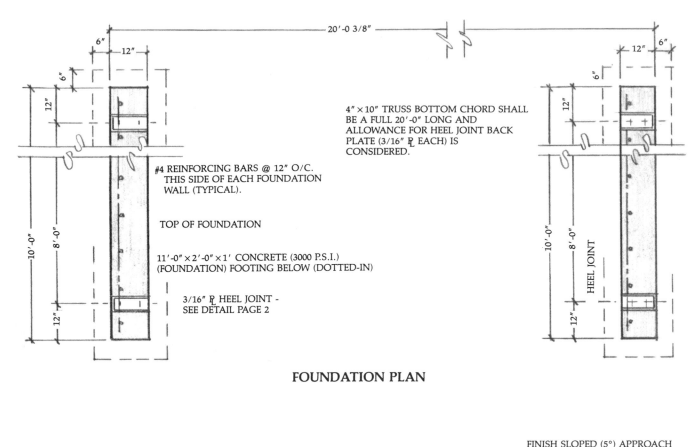

4" × 10" TRUSS BOTTOM CHORD SHALL BE A FULL 20'-0" LONG AND ALLOWANCE FOR HEEL JOINT BACK PLATE (3/16" ₽ EACH) IS CONSIDERED.

#4 REINFORCING BARS @ 12" O/C. THIS SIDE OF EACH FOUNDATION WALL (TYPICAL).

TOP OF FOUNDATION

11'-0" × 2'-0" × 1' CONCRETE (3000 P.S.I.) (FOUNDATION) FOOTING BELOW (DOTTED-IN)

3/16" ₽ HEEL JOINT - SEE DETAIL PAGE 2

FOUNDATION PLAN

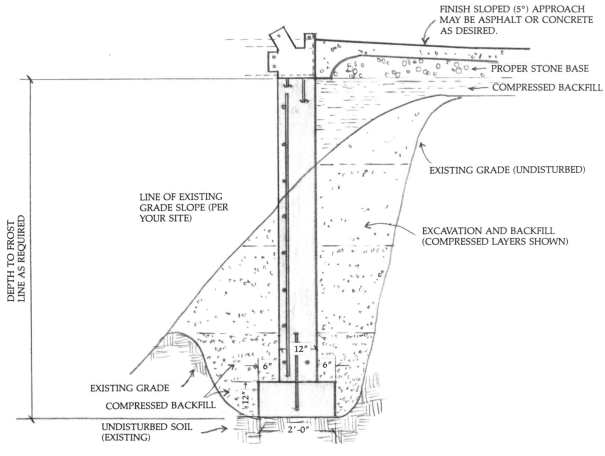

FINISH SLOPED (5°) APPROACH MAY BE ASPHALT OR CONCRETE AS DESIRED.

PROPER STONE BASE

COMPRESSED BACKFILL

EXISTING GRADE (UNDISTURBED)

EXCAVATION AND BACKFILL (COMPRESSED LAYERS SHOWN)

DEPTH TO FROST LINE AS REQUIRED

LINE OF EXISTING GRADE SLOPE (PER YOUR SITE)

EXISTING GRADE

COMPRESSED BACKFILL

UNDISTURBED SOIL (EXISTING)

NOTES:
—ADDITIONAL SHORING AND RETAINING WALLS (SUCH AS CONCRETE OR STONE) MAY BE NECESSARY PER YOUR SITE.

FOUNDATION PROFILE

NIAGARA

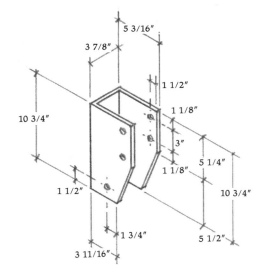

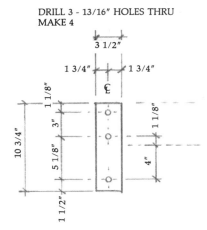

DRILL 3 - 13/16" HOLES THRU
MAKE 4

WELD TOGETHER 3-℔ PIECES.
ALL CORNERS SQUARE UNLESS NOTED.
DRILL 6 - 13/16" Ø HOLES THRU IN
   IDENTICAL PATTERN AS SHOWN.

℔ DETAIL A

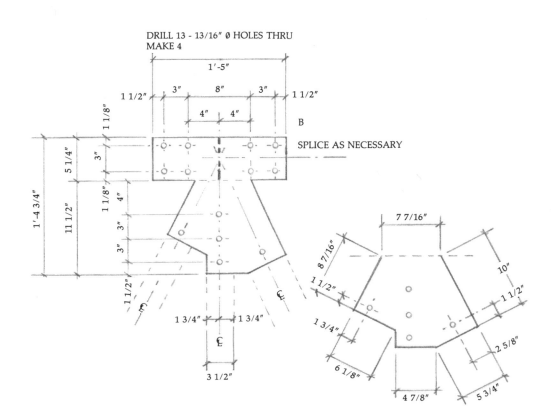

DRILL 13 - 13/16" Ø HOLES THRU
MAKE 4

SPLICE AS NECESSARY

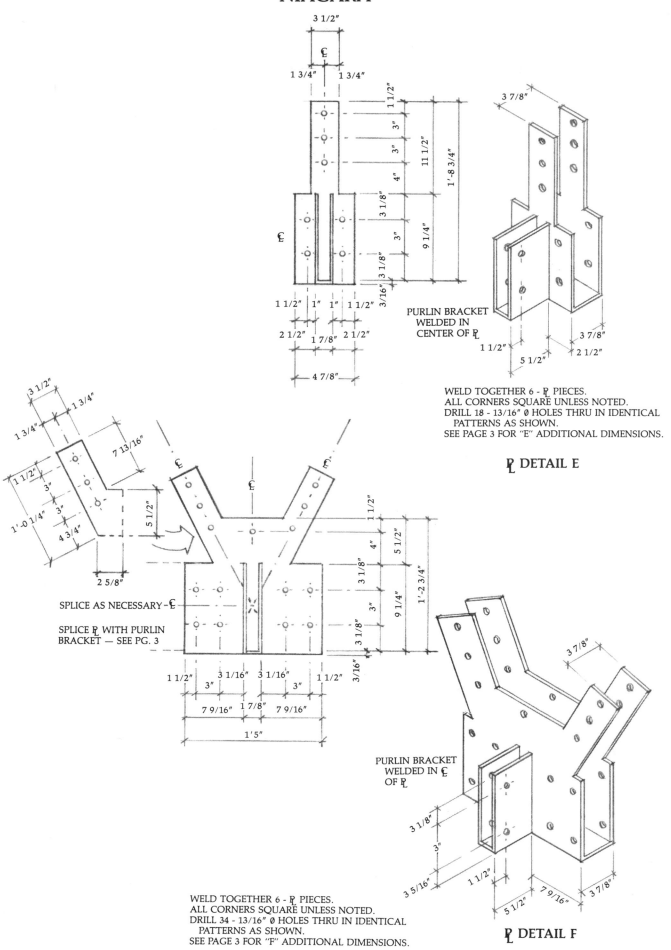

PURLIN BRACKET
WELDED IN
CENTER OF ℄

WELD TOGETHER 6 - ℄ PIECES.
ALL CORNERS SQUARE UNLESS NOTED.
DRILL 18 - 13/16″ Ø HOLES THRU IN IDENTICAL
PATTERNS AS SHOWN.
SEE PAGE 3 FOR "E" ADDITIONAL DIMENSIONS.

℄ DETAIL E

SPLICE AS NECESSARY - ℄

SPLICE ℄ WITH PURLIN
BRACKET — SEE PG. 3

PURLIN BRACKET
WELDED IN ℄
OF ℄

WELD TOGETHER 6 - ℄ PIECES.
ALL CORNERS SQUARE UNLESS NOTED.
DRILL 34 - 13/16″ Ø HOLES THRU IN IDENTICAL
PATTERNS AS SHOWN.
SEE PAGE 3 FOR "F" ADDITIONAL DIMENSIONS.

℄ DETAIL F

NIAGARA

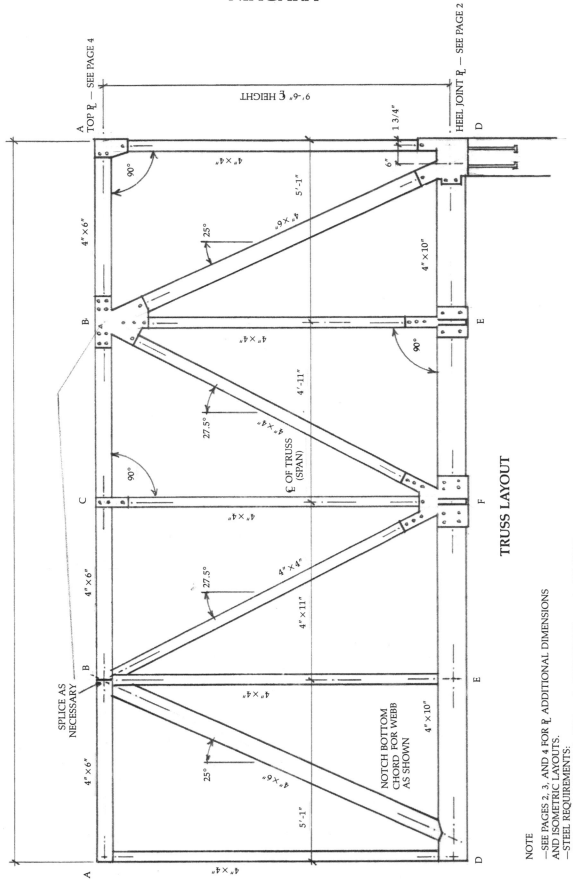

TRUSS LAYOUT

NOTE

—SEE PAGES 2, 3, AND 4 FOR ℞ ADDITIONAL DIMENSIONS
AND ISOMETRIC LAYOUTS.

—STEEL REQUIREMENTS:

USE 3/16" ℞ (MINIMUM). AND 3/4" ∅ BOLTS WITH 1 1/2" ∅ WASHERS.

DRILL 13/16" ∅ HOLES AS SHOWN.

ALL CORNERS SQUARE UNLESS NOTED.

NOTICE THAT ₵ OF TRUSS MEMBERS MEET AND ARE
LAYOUT GUIDES ("B" AND "F").

REMEMBER TO DOUBLE THE NUMBER OF ℞ CONNECTIONS
DRAWN (ONE EACH SIDE OF WOOD MEMBERS) "B" AND "C".

NIAGARA

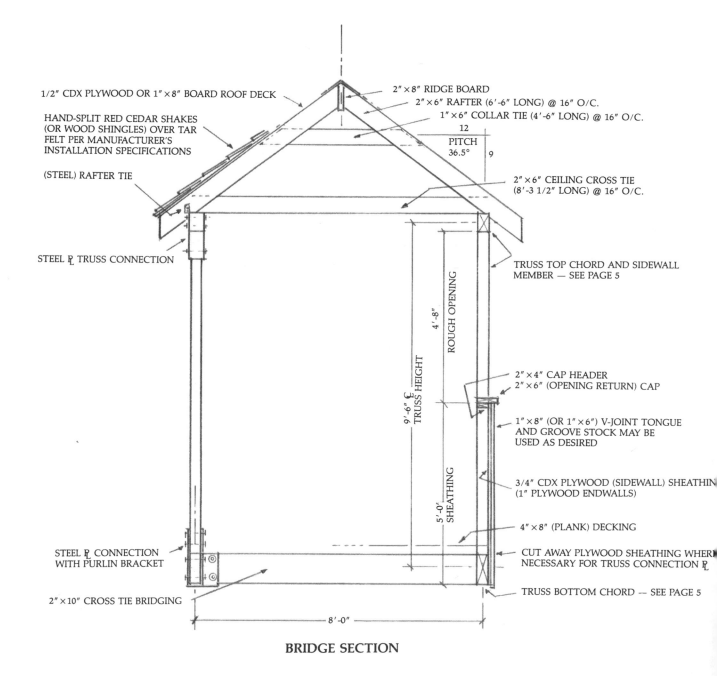

1/2" CDX PLYWOOD OR 1"×8" BOARD ROOF DECK

HAND-SPLIT RED CEDAR SHAKES (OR WOOD SHINGLES) OVER TAR FELT PER MANUFACTURER'S INSTALLATION SPECIFICATIONS

(STEEL) RAFTER TIE

STEEL ₽ TRUSS CONNECTION

2"×8" RIDGE BOARD

2"×6" RAFTER (6'-6" LONG) @ 16" O/C.

1"×6" COLLAR TIE (4'-6" LONG) @ 16" O/C.

12

PITCH 36.5°   9

2"×6" CEILING CROSS TIE (8'-3 1/2" LONG) @ 16" O/C.

TRUSS TOP CHORD AND SIDEWALL MEMBER — SEE PAGE 5

ROUGH OPENING

4'-8"

9'-6" ₵ TRUSS HEIGHT

2"×4" CAP HEADER
2"×6" (OPENING RETURN) CAP

1"×8" (OR 1"×6") V-JOINT TONGUE AND GROOVE STOCK MAY BE USED AS DESIRED

3/4" CDX PLYWOOD (SIDEWALL) SHEATHING (1" PLYWOOD ENDWALLS)

5'-0" SHEATHING

4"×8" (PLANK) DECKING

STEEL ₽ CONNECTION WITH PURLIN BRACKET

CUT AWAY PLYWOOD SHEATHING WHERE NECESSARY FOR TRUSS CONNECTION ₽

TRUSS BOTTOM CHORD — SEE PAGE 5

2"×10" CROSS TIE BRIDGING

8'-0"

BRIDGE SECTION

NIAGARA

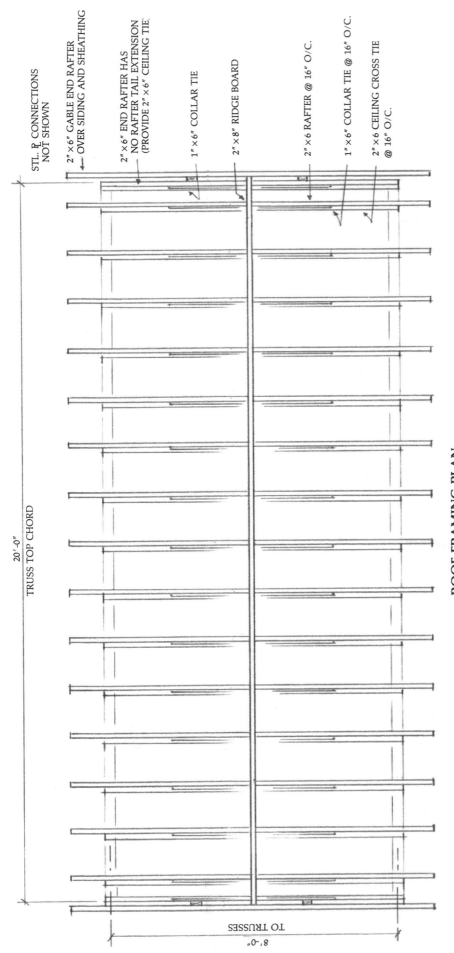

ROOF FRAMING PLAN

STL. ₽ CONNECTIONS NOT SHOWN

2" × 6" GABLE END RAFTER OVER SIDING AND SHEATHING

2" × 6" END RAFTER HAS NO RAFTER TAIL EXTENSION (PROVIDE 2" × 6" CEILING TIE)

1" × 6" COLLAR TIE

2" × 8" RIDGE BOARD

2" × 6 RAFTER @ 16" O/C.

1" × 6" COLLAR TIE @ 16" O/C.

2" × 6 CEILING CROSS TIE @ 16" O/C.

20'-0" TRUSS TOP CHORD

T/O TRUSSES

8'-0"

—SUGGESTED PROCEDURE—

CONSTRUCT FOOTINGS AND FOUNDATIONS AS OUTLINED, SETTING 4 - HEEL JOINTS ANCHOR BOLTS IN FRESHLY POURED CONCRETE FOUNDATION TOPS. MEASURE CAREFULLY.
SET AND ANCHOR 2 - MAIN SPAN TRUSSES (CONCRETE TO CURE 7 - DAYS). IF TRUSSES ARE BUILT IN PLACE, A MINIMUM LOAD PARTIAL WORK DECK MAY BE CON— STRUCTED AFTER PURLIN TIES ARE COMPLETED. BRACE SIDEWALL TRUSSES TEMPORARILY AS REQUIRED. COMPLETE DECK PLANKING AND CEILING CROSS TIES. BUILD ROOF RAFTERS (STATE APPROVED TRUSSES MAY BE USED). ADD TIES. GABLE END (RAFTERS), ROOF DECK, TAR FELT, AND SHINGLES. ADD WALL SHEATHING WITH OPENINGS PROVIDED. ADD SIDING, CAP BOARDS, AND TRIM.

93

NIAGARA

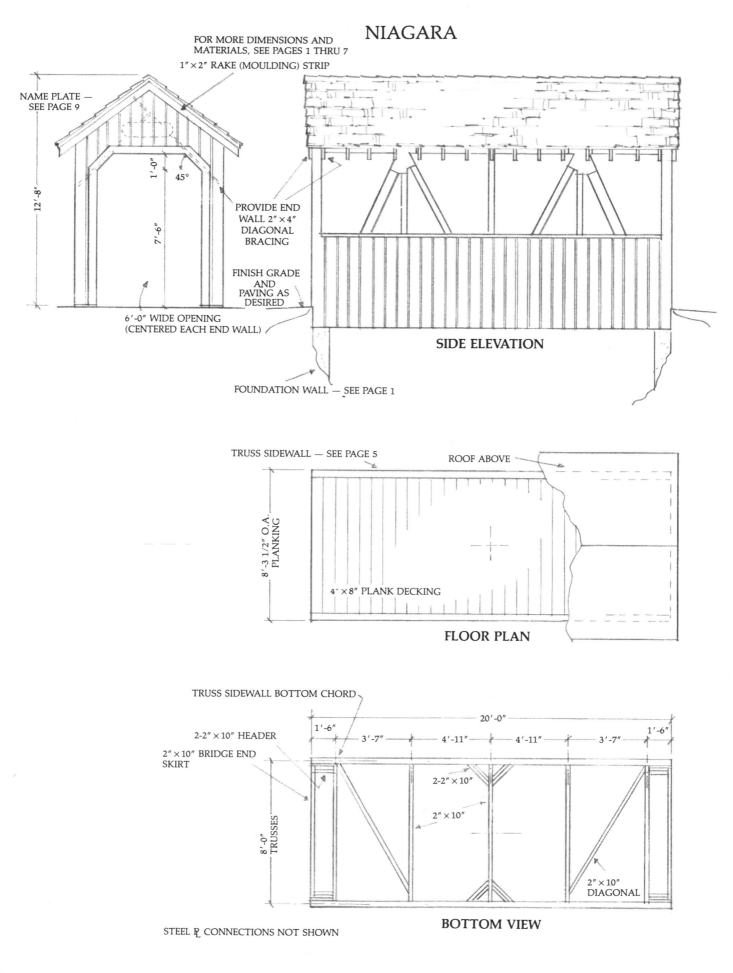

FOR MORE DIMENSIONS AND MATERIALS, SEE PAGES 1 THRU 7

1" × 2" RAKE (MOULDING) STRIP

NAME PLATE — SEE PAGE 9

12'-8"

1'-0"

45°

7'-6"

PROVIDE END WALL 2" × 4" DIAGONAL BRACING

FINISH GRADE AND PAVING AS DESIRED

6'-0" WIDE OPENING (CENTERED EACH END WALL)

FOUNDATION WALL — SEE PAGE 1

SIDE ELEVATION

TRUSS SIDEWALL — SEE PAGE 5

ROOF ABOVE

8'-3 1/2" O.A. PLANKING

4" × 8" PLANK DECKING

FLOOR PLAN

TRUSS SIDEWALL BOTTOM CHORD

2-2" × 10" HEADER

2" × 10" BRIDGE END SKIRT

20'-0"

1'-6"   3'-7"   4'-11"   4'-11"   3'-7"   1'-6"

2-2" × 10"

2" × 10"

8'-0" TRUSSES

2" × 10" DIAGONAL

BOTTOM VIEW

STEEL ℔ CONNECTIONS NOT SHOWN

CUPOLA PLANS

GENERAL INFORMATION FOR CUPOLA CONSTRUCTION AND DESIGN NOTES

We believe these general recommendations to be good advice and should be followed when building a cupola.

Nailing and bracing not detailed here should be according to good construction practice. If you have questions, do not hesitate to consult an experienced carpenter.

All work should be done in a workmanlike manner and care should be taken to see that all parts are properly nailed, fastened or fitted. Double check all of your measurements before you do any cutting. The wood dimensions given are nominal (not actual). For example a $2'' \times 4''$'s actual dimensions are $1^1/_2'' \times 3^1/_2''$. The full size moulding section are only suggestions — stock substitutes may be made.

It is advisable to build the cupola in your workshop and then arrange for help to install it on your roof. Do not remove roof shingles or cut into roof until you are ready to install the cupola and the weather is clear. After removing shingles from the installation work area, apply 15# roofing paper even if some still exists on the roof deck. Shingles may be replaced later where needed. Remove shingles carefully for reuse.

If the cupola is built in your workshop and then lifted into place on the roof, attach $2'' \times 4''$ horizontal plates (see drawings) on the roof, on each side of the ridge. These will help locate the new cupola for proper anchoring. Remember, measure accurately.

Do not attach siding to the cupola skirt in shop. Wait until after the cupola frame is properly anchored to the roof, for easy access to roof and anchoring members. (Use a 4" lag bolt minimum.)

Apply a soldered metal flashing (i.e. 28 gauge galvanized metal) over the 15# roofing paper where the new cupola meets the existing roof. Apply one side under the cupola skirt and the other side of the flashing on top of the shingles. The flashing, 12" wide and bent to an L shape, with 6" on either side of the bend, is the minimum size for proper rain runoff.

If the new cupola will be required to exhaust air from the building, some precautions and suggestions should be considered, such as:
A. Provide a vertical soldered metal riser around the area opening in the existing roof after applying 15# roof paper as noted above and the rise should be at least 4" above the roof.
B. A stationary metal louvre and bird screen (local building supply store) should be installed. The inside dimension of the cupola will determine the louvre size, and the louvre size will determine the new opening size to cut in the roof. Screening will also be needed behind louvres on wall open-style louvres. Use roofing compound/silicone sealer, etc., to achieve a tight seal around screens and flashings to prevent leaks.

Remember, cutting into any structural roof can lead to problems if practical common sense is not used. All outdoor wood structures are subject to varying weather conditions. To prolong their life, it is advisable to use good quality products throughout including stain, paint, waterproof glue and of course, galvanized nails, screws and bolts where required.

PENNSYLVANIA

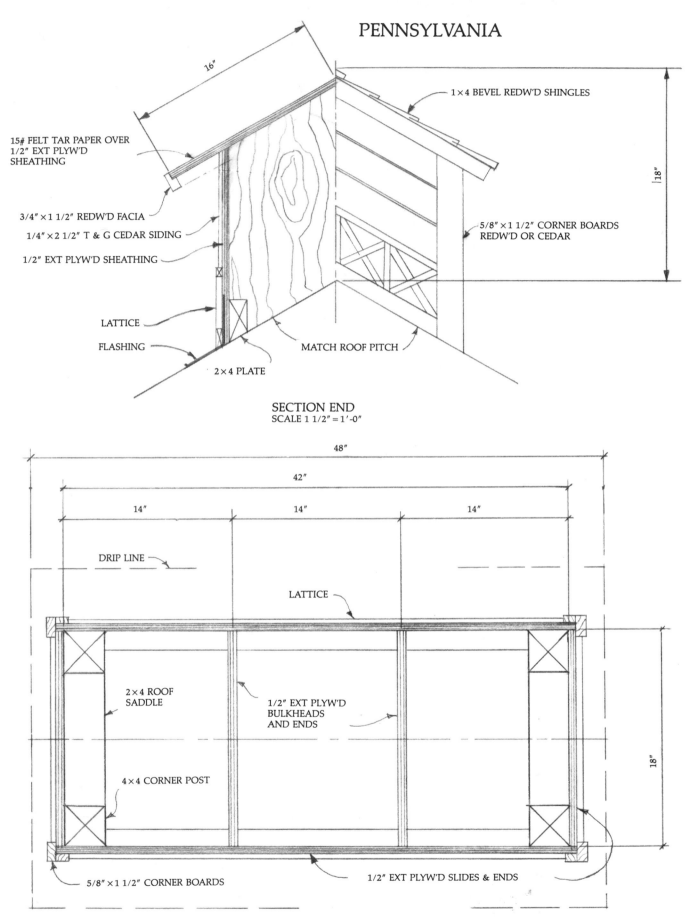

16"

15# FELT TAR PAPER OVER
1/2" EXT PLYW'D
SHEATHING

1 × 4 BEVEL REDW'D SHINGLES

18"

3/4" × 1 1/2" REDW'D FACIA

1/4" × 2 1/2" T & G CEDAR SIDING

1/2" EXT PLYW'D SHEATHING

5/8" × 1 1/2" CORNER BOARDS
REDW'D OR CEDAR

LATTICE

FLASHING

MATCH ROOF PITCH

2 × 4 PLATE

SECTION END
SCALE 1 1/2" = 1'-0"

48"

42"

14"   14"   14"

DRIP LINE

LATTICE

2 × 4 ROOF
SADDLE

1/2" EXT PLYW'D
BULKHEADS
AND ENDS

18"

4 × 4 CORNER POST

5/8" × 1 1/2" CORNER BOARDS

1/2" EXT PLYW'D SLIDES & ENDS

PLAN VIEW SCALE 1 1/2" = 1'-0"

PENNSYLVANIA

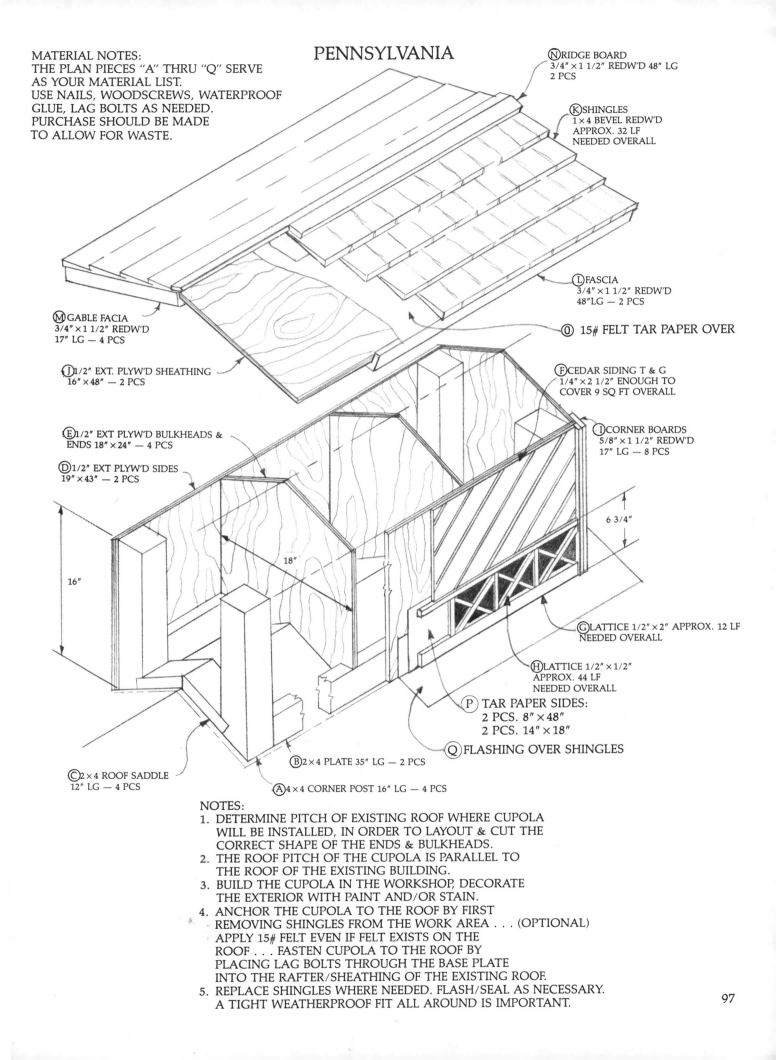

MATERIAL NOTES:
THE PLAN PIECES "A" THRU "Q" SERVE
AS YOUR MATERIAL LIST.
USE NAILS, WOODSCREWS, WATERPROOF
GLUE, LAG BOLTS AS NEEDED.
PURCHASE SHOULD BE MADE
TO ALLOW FOR WASTE.

(N) RIDGE BOARD
3/4" × 1 1/2" REDW'D 48" LG
2 PCS

(K) SHINGLES
1 × 4 BEVEL REDW'D
APPROX. 32 LF
NEEDED OVERALL

(L) FASCIA
3/4" × 1 1/2" REDW'D
48" LG — 2 PCS

(M) GABLE FACIA
3/4" × 1 1/2" REDW'D
17" LG — 4 PCS

(J) 1/2" EXT. PLYW'D SHEATHING
16" × 48" — 2 PCS

(O) 15# FELT TAR PAPER OVER

(F) CEDAR SIDING T & G
1/4" × 2 1/2" ENOUGH TO
COVER 9 SQ FT OVERALL

(E) 1/2" EXT PLYW'D BULKHEADS &
ENDS 18" × 24" — 4 PCS

(I) CORNER BOARDS
5/8" × 1 1/2" REDW'D
17" LG — 8 PCS

(D) 1/2" EXT PLYW'D SIDES
19" × 43" — 2 PCS

6 3/4"

18"

16"

(G) LATTICE 1/2" × 2" APPROX. 12 LF
NEEDED OVERALL

(H) LATTICE 1/2" × 1/2"
APPROX. 44 LF
NEEDED OVERALL

(P) TAR PAPER SIDES:
2 PCS. 8" × 48"
2 PCS. 14" × 18"

(Q) FLASHING OVER SHINGLES

(B) 2 × 4 PLATE 35" LG — 2 PCS

(C) 2 × 4 ROOF SADDLE
12" LG — 4 PCS

(A) 4 × 4 CORNER POST 16" LG — 4 PCS

NOTES:
1. DETERMINE PITCH OF EXISTING ROOF WHERE CUPOLA
   WILL BE INSTALLED, IN ORDER TO LAYOUT & CUT THE
   CORRECT SHAPE OF THE ENDS & BULKHEADS.
2. THE ROOF PITCH OF THE CUPOLA IS PARALLEL TO
   THE ROOF OF THE EXISTING BUILDING.
3. BUILD THE CUPOLA IN THE WORKSHOP, DECORATE
   THE EXTERIOR WITH PAINT AND/OR STAIN.
4. ANCHOR THE CUPOLA TO THE ROOF BY FIRST
   REMOVING SHINGLES FROM THE WORK AREA . . . (OPTIONAL)
   APPLY 15# FELT EVEN IF FELT EXISTS ON THE
   ROOF . . . FASTEN CUPOLA TO THE ROOF BY
   PLACING LAG BOLTS THROUGH THE BASE PLATE
   INTO THE RAFTER/SHEATHING OF THE EXISTING ROOF.
5. REPLACE SHINGLES WHERE NEEDED. FLASH/SEAL AS NECESSARY.
   A TIGHT WEATHERPROOF FIT ALL AROUND IS IMPORTANT.

BROOKLYN

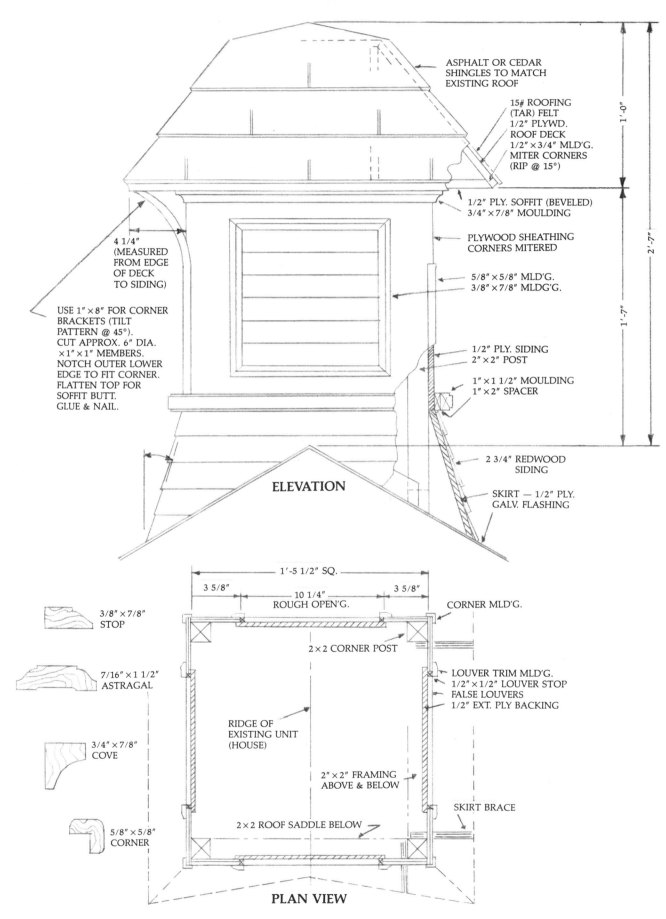

ASPHALT OR CEDAR
SHINGLES TO MATCH
EXISTING ROOF

15# ROOFING
(TAR) FELT
1/2" PLYWD.
ROOF DECK
1/2" × 3/4" MLD'G.
MITER CORNERS
(RIP @ 15°)

1/2" PLY. SOFFIT (BEVELED)
3/4" × 7/8" MOULDING

PLYWOOD SHEATHING
CORNERS MITERED

5/8" × 5/8" MLD'G.
3/8" × 7/8" MLDG'G.

1/2" PLY. SIDING
2" × 2" POST

1" × 1 1/2" MOULDING
1" × 2" SPACER

2 3/4" REDWOOD
SIDING

SKIRT — 1/2" PLY.
GALV. FLASHING

1'-0"

2'-7"

1'-7"

4 1/4"
(MEASURED
FROM EDGE
OF DECK
TO SIDING)

USE 1" × 8" FOR CORNER
BRACKETS (TILT
PATTERN @ 45°).
CUT APPROX. 6" DIA.
× 1" × 1" MEMBERS.
NOTCH OUTER LOWER
EDGE TO FIT CORNER.
FLATTEN TOP FOR
SOFFIT BUTT.
GLUE & NAIL.

ELEVATION

3/8" × 7/8"
STOP

7/16" × 1 1/2"
ASTRAGAL

3/4" × 7/8"
COVE

5/8" × 5/8"
CORNER

1'-5 1/2" SQ.

3 5/8"

10 1/4"
ROUGH OPEN'G.

3 5/8"

CORNER MLD'G.

2×2 CORNER POST

LOUVER TRIM MLD'G.
1/2" × 1/2" LOUVER STOP
FALSE LOUVERS
1/2" EXT. PLY BACKING

RIDGE OF
EXISTING UNIT
(HOUSE)

2" × 2" FRAMING
ABOVE & BELOW

SKIRT BRACE

2 × 2 ROOF SADDLE BELOW

PLAN VIEW

BROOKLYN

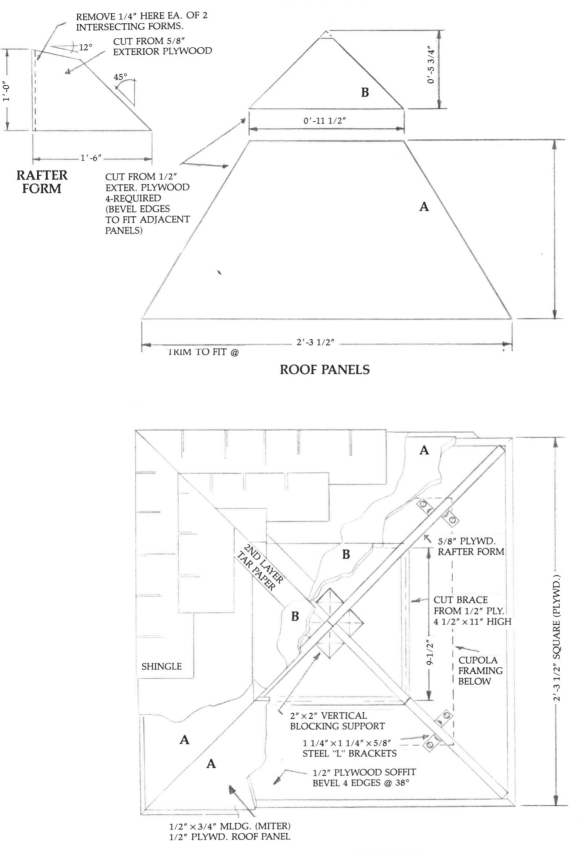

REMOVE 1/4" HERE EA. OF 2 INTERSECTING FORMS.

CUT FROM 5/8" EXTERIOR PLYWOOD

12°

45°

1'-0"

1'-6"

RAFTER FORM

CUT FROM 1/2" EXTER. PLYWOOD 4-REQUIRED (BEVEL EDGES TO FIT ADJACENT PANELS)

B

0'-5 3/4"

0'-11 1/2"

A

2'-3 1/2"

TRIM TO FIT @

ROOF PANELS

2ND LAYER TAR PAPER

A

B

B

B

SHINGLE

A

A

A

5/8" PLYWD. RAFTER FORM

CUT BRACE FROM 1/2" PLY. 4 1/2" × 11" HIGH

CUPOLA FRAMING BELOW

9-1/2"

2'-3 1/2" SQUARE (PLYWD.)

2" × 2" VERTICAL BLOCKING SUPPORT

1 1/4" × 1 1/4" × 5/8" STEEL "L" BRACKETS

1/2" PLYWOOD SOFFIT BEVEL 4 EDGES @ 38°

1/2" × 3/4" MLDG. (MITER)
1/2" PLYWD. ROOF PANEL

ROOF FRAMING PLAN

BROOKLYN

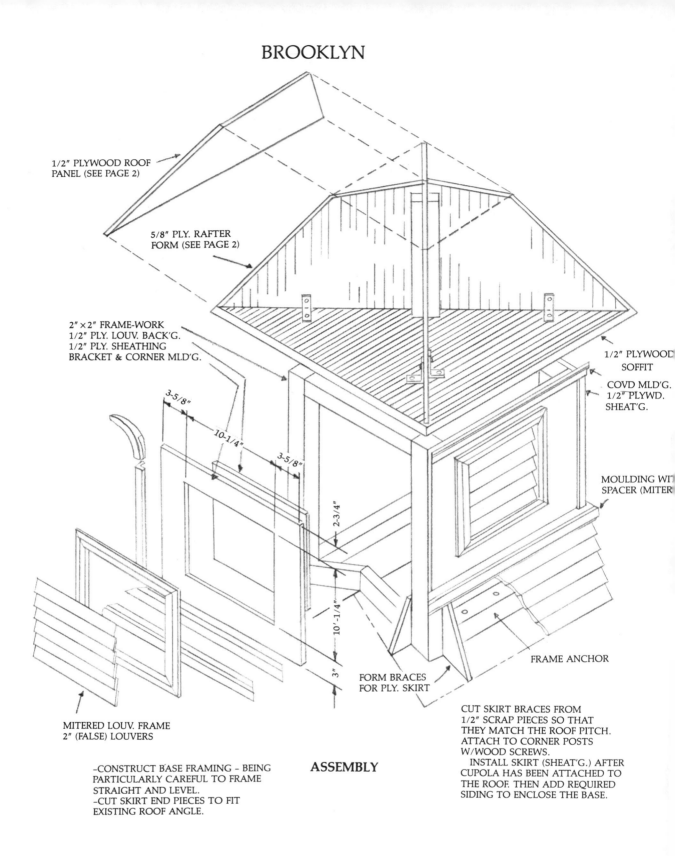

1/2" PLYWOOD ROOF PANEL (SEE PAGE 2)

5/8" PLY. RAFTER FORM (SEE PAGE 2)

2" × 2" FRAME-WORK
1/2" PLY. LOUV. BACK'G.
1/2" PLY. SHEATHING
BRACKET & CORNER MLD'G.

1/2" PLYWOOD SOFFIT

COVD MLD'G.
1/2" PLYWD. SHEAT'G.

MOULDING WIT
SPACER (MITER

3-5/8"

10-1/4"

3-5/8"

2-3/4"

10'-1/4"

3"

MOULDING WIT
SPACER (MITER

FRAME ANCHOR

FORM BRACES FOR PLY. SKIRT

MITERED LOUV. FRAME
2" (FALSE) LOUVERS

–CONSTRUCT BASE FRAMING – BEING PARTICULARLY CAREFUL TO FRAME STRAIGHT AND LEVEL.
–CUT SKIRT END PIECES TO FIT EXISTING ROOF ANGLE.

ASSEMBLY

CUT SKIRT BRACES FROM 1/2" SCRAP PIECES SO THAT THEY MATCH THE ROOF PITCH. ATTACH TO CORNER POSTS W/WOOD SCREWS.
    INSTALL SKIRT (SHEAT'G.) AFTER CUPOLA HAS BEEN ATTACHED TO THE ROOF. THEN ADD REQUIRED SIDING TO ENCLOSE THE BASE.

BROOKLYN

OPTIONAL CONSTRUCTION

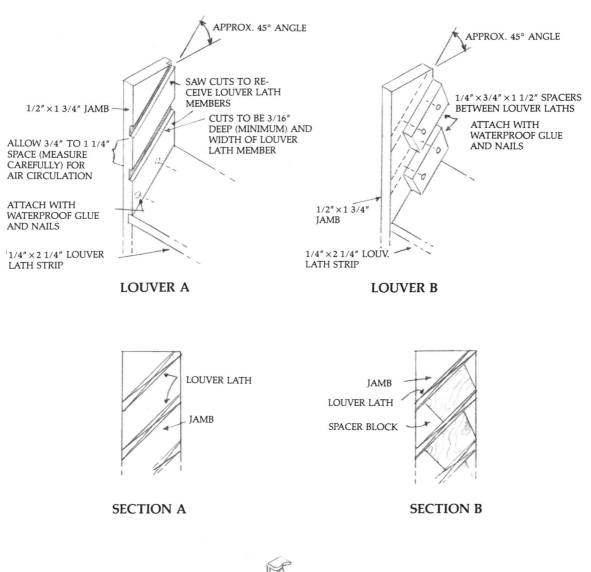

APPROX. 45° ANGLE

SAW CUTS TO RE-
CEIVE LOUVER LATH
MEMBERS

1/2" × 1 3/4" JAMB

CUTS TO BE 3/16"
DEEP (MINIMUM) AND
WIDTH OF LOUVER
LATH MEMBER

ALLOW 3/4" TO 1 1/4"
SPACE (MEASURE
CAREFULLY) FOR
AIR CIRCULATION

ATTACH WITH
WATERPROOF GLUE
AND NAILS

1/4" × 2 1/4" LOUVER
LATH STRIP

LOUVER A

APPROX. 45° ANGLE

1/4" × 3/4" × 1 1/2" SPACERS
BETWEEN LOUVER LATHS

ATTACH WITH
WATERPROOF GLUE
AND NAILS

1/2" × 1 3/4"
JAMB

1/4" × 2 1/4" LOUV.
LATH STRIP

LOUVER B

LOUVER LATH

JAMB

SECTION A

JAMB

LOUVER LATH

SPACER BLOCK

SECTION B

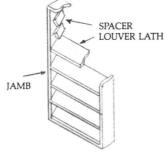

SPACER
LOUVER LATH

JAMB

ISOMETRIC B

BROOKLYN

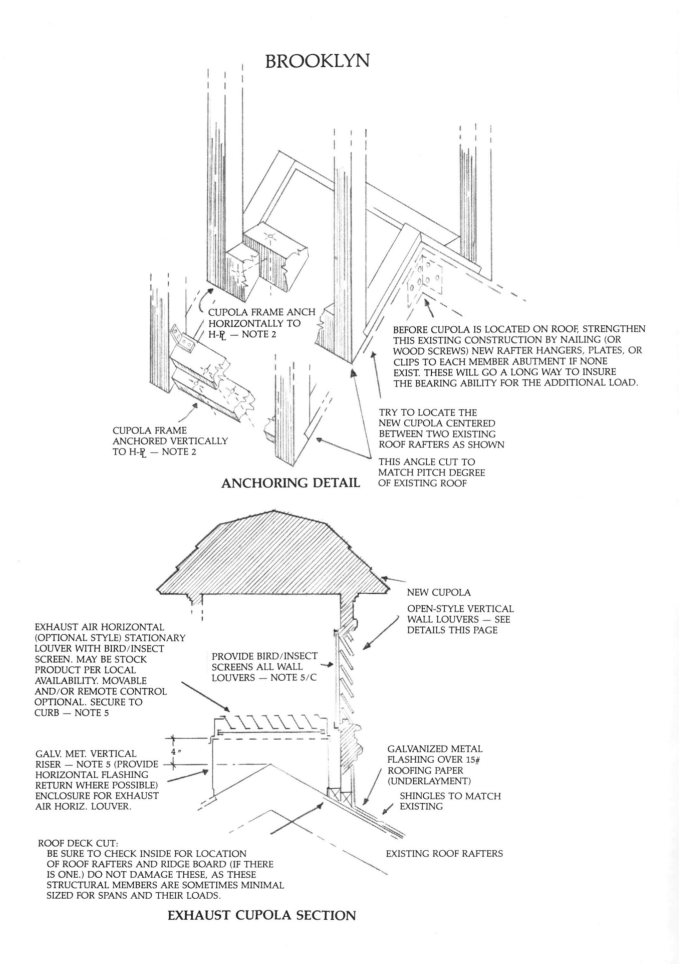

CUPOLA FRAME ANCH
HORIZONTALLY TO
H-P — NOTE 2

BEFORE CUPOLA IS LOCATED ON ROOF, STRENGTHEN
THIS EXISTING CONSTRUCTION BY NAILING (OR
WOOD SCREWS) NEW RAFTER HANGERS, PLATES, OR
CLIPS TO EACH MEMBER ABUTMENT IF NONE
EXIST. THESE WILL GO A LONG WAY TO INSURE
THE BEARING ABILITY FOR THE ADDITIONAL LOAD.

CUPOLA FRAME
ANCHORED VERTICALLY
TO H-P — NOTE 2

TRY TO LOCATE THE
NEW CUPOLA CENTERED
BETWEEN TWO EXISTING
ROOF RAFTERS AS SHOWN

THIS ANGLE CUT TO
MATCH PITCH DEGREE
OF EXISTING ROOF

ANCHORING DETAIL

NEW CUPOLA

OPEN-STYLE VERTICAL
WALL LOUVERS — SEE
DETAILS THIS PAGE

EXHAUST AIR HORIZONTAL
(OPTIONAL STYLE) STATIONARY
LOUVER WITH BIRD/INSECT
SCREEN. MAY BE STOCK
PRODUCT PER LOCAL
AVAILABILITY. MOVABLE
AND/OR REMOTE CONTROL
OPTIONAL. SECURE TO
CURB — NOTE 5

PROVIDE BIRD/INSECT
SCREENS ALL WALL
LOUVERS — NOTE 5/C

GALV. MET. VERTICAL
RISER — NOTE 5 (PROVIDE
HORIZONTAL FLASHING
RETURN WHERE POSSIBLE)
ENCLOSURE FOR EXHAUST
AIR HORIZ. LOUVER.

4"

GALVANIZED METAL
FLASHING OVER 15#
ROOFING PAPER
(UNDERLAYMENT)

SHINGLES TO MATCH
EXISTING

ROOF DECK CUT:
BE SURE TO CHECK INSIDE FOR LOCATION
OF ROOF RAFTERS AND RIDGE BOARD (IF THERE
IS ONE.) DO NOT DAMAGE THESE, AS THESE
STRUCTURAL MEMBERS ARE SOMETIMES MINIMAL
SIZED FOR SPANS AND THEIR LOADS.

EXISTING ROOF RAFTERS

EXHAUST CUPOLA SECTION

BROOKLYN

MATERIALS REQUIRED:

1/2" EXTERIOR PLYWOOD (ROOF PANELS, SOFFIT, SHEATHING, LOUVER BACKING AND SKIRTS)		2 SHT.
5/8" EXTERIOR PLYWOOD (ROOF RAFTER FORMS)		1/2 SHT.
2" × 2" FIR (FRAMING AND ANCHORS)		24 LF.
1/2" × 3/4"	CLEAR PINE MOULDING (ROOF DECK EDGE)	9 LF
3/8" × 7/8"	CLEAR PINE MOULDING (LOUVER TRIM)	16 LF
5/8" × 5/8"	CLEAR PINE MOULDING (CORNERS)	3 LF
3/4" × 7/8"	CLEAR PINE MOULDING (COVE)	6 LF
7/16" × 1 1/2"	CLEAR PINE MOULDING (ASTRAGAL)	7 LF
1" × 2"	CLEAR PINE MOULDING (ASTRAGAL SPACER)	7 LF
1/2" × 1/2"	CLEAR PINE MOULDING (LOUVER STOP)	16 LF
1" × 8"	CLEAR PINE (SOFFIT CORNER BRACKET)	3 LF
SHINGLES (WOOD OR ASPHALT STRIP)		9 SF
15 LB. ROOFING TAR FELT		9 SF
2 3/4" REDWOOD SIDING (SKIRT)		30 LF
GALV. SHEET METAL SKIRT PERIMETER FLASHING		9 LF
1 1/4" × 1 1/4" × 5/8" STEEL ANCHOR BRACKETS		8 EA

ADD 10% TO 20% TO THE ROUGH LUMBER ESTIMATES FOR WASTE.
FINISH WOOD WASTE (PINE TRIM) WILL BE MINIMAL.

SHEET METAL ROOF CAP (OPTIONAL)
4 ROOF RIDGES: USE EXTRA
LAYER OF TAR PAPER UNDER
SHINGLES (FIT CAREFULLY)

CONSTRUCTION NOTES:

1. REMOVE SHINGLES (OPTIONAL) FROM INSTALLATION WORK AREA. THEN APPLY ROOFING (TAR) PAPER EVEN IF PAPER EXISTS ON ROOF DECK. REPLACE SHINGLES LATER WHERE NEEDED.
2. IF COMPLETE CUPOLA IS BUILT ON THE GROUND AND THEN LIFTED INTO PLACE, ATTACH 2" × 4" HORIZONTAL PLATES (H-P.-SEE DRWGS.) ON ROOF, EACH SIDE OF RIDGE. THESE WILL HELP LOCATE THE NEW CUPOLA FOR PROPER ANCHORING. MEASURE ACCURATELY. SEE NOTE 3.
3. IF COMPLETE CUPOLA IS LIFTED TO ROOF TO BE ANCHORED, DO NOT ATTACH SKIRT SIDING (SEE DRWGS.) UNTIL AFTER THE CUPOLA FRAME IS PROPERLY ANCHORED (4" LONG MIN. LAG BOLTS).
4. FOR EXTRA PROTECTION APPLY SOLDERED METAL FLASHING (IE. GALVANIZED 28 GA.) OVER 15# ROOFING PAPER WHERE THE NEW CUPOLA MEETS THE EXISTING ROOF. APPLY UNDER CUPOLA SKIRT SIDING AND ON TOP OF SHINGLES. 12" WIDE METAL FLASHING WILL PROVIDE 6" OF COVER ON EACH SURFACE (MINIMUM FOR PROPER RAIN RUNOFF).
5. IF THE NEW CUPOLA WILL BE REQUIRED TO EXHAUST AIR FROM THE BUILDING, SOME PRECAUTIONS AND SUGGESTIONS SHOULD BE CONSIDERED: A. PROVIDE A VERTICAL SOLDERED METAL RISER AROUND THE NEW OPENING IN THE EXISTING ROOF (APPLY ROOFING PAPER PER NOTE 1 FIRST). THE RISER SHOULD BE AT LEAST 4" IN HEIGHT. B. A STATIONARY METAL LOUVER AND BIRD SCREEN, PROBABLY STOCK COMPONENTS, SHOULD BE INSTALLED. THE INSIDE DIMENSION OF THE CUPOLA WILL DETERMINE THE LOUVER SIZE, AND THE LOUVER SIZE WILL DETERMINE THE ROOF (NEW) OPENING SIZE. C. CUPOLA WALL OPEN-STYLE LOUVERS (SEE DETAILS THIS PAGE) AND BIRD/INSECT SCREENS FOR THESE OPEN LOUVERS WILL BE REQUIRED. D. NEEDLESS TO SAY, A TIGHT SEAL AROUND SCREENS AND STURDY STANDARD CONSTRUCTION PRACTICE OVERALL IS QUITE IMPORTANT. CUTTING INTO ANY STRUCTURAL ROOF CAN LEAD TO PROBLEMS IF PRACTICAL COMMON SENSE IS NOT USED.

CUPOLA PLAN PRICE LIST

NEW YORKER
HORICON
LENINGRAD
MINNESOTA
OREGON
KANSAS
CHICAGO
WYOMING
HAMPSHIRE
GEORGIAN
CAPISTRANO
KENTUCKY
NEVADA
NEW ORLEANS
SEATTLE
COPENHAGEN
IDAHO
INDIANA
BROOKLYN
DAKOTA
PENNSYLVANIA
SANTA FE
CHARLESTON
WASHINGTON
VERMONT
FLORIDA.............6.95 PPD each design

TELEMARK
CAROLINA
ONTARIO
JERSEY
WISCONSIN
INDEPENDENCE
MARTIN HOUSE
BOSTON
ALBERTA
MANDARIN...........8.95 PPD each design

GAZEBOS & OTHER GARDEN
STRUCTURES ....7.95 PPD

PRIVY — THE CLASSIC OUTHOUSE
BOOK ....7.95 PPD

STROM TOYS
(Full Color) 9.95

BRIDGE PLAN PRICE LIST

PLATTE .... 7.50 PPD

NORTH FORK .... 12.95 PPD

ROGUE
RUBICON
BRITTANY
SACRAMENTO
SAVANNAH
ALLEGHENY
SUMIDA
TAI-PAN ....14.95 PPD each design

MOHAWK
POTOMAC
SHENANDOAH
SWEETWATER
YUKON
WABASH
TENNESSEE
COLUMBIA
BIG SANDY DRAWBRIDGE
ST. CROIX
CHATTAHOOCHEE .....22.95 PPD each design

SWANEE
MISSISSIPPI
SUSQUEHANNA
HUDSON
NIAGARA
DELAWARE............27.95 PPD each design

RIO GRANDE ....32.95 PPD

CUMBERLAND ....37.95 PPD

Check, money order, MasterCard or Visa **with order.**
Please include account number and expiration date
with charge orders. **Wisconsin** residents add 5% sales
tax.

Send orders to: **SUN DESIGNS**
P.O. Box 206
Delafield, WI 53018